DAY BY DAY WITH DAVID

Devotional Studies in 1st and 2nd Samuel, Psalms

TOMMIE MCBRAYER

WESTBOW
PRESS®
A DIVISION OF THOMAS NELSON
& ZONDERVAN

WestBow Press books may be ordered through booksellers or by contacting:

WestBow Press
A Division of Thomas Nelson & Zondervan
1663 Liberty Drive
Bloomington, IN 47403
www.westbowpress.com
844-714-3454

Unless otherwise stated, all scripture is taken from the New King James Version, Thomas Nelson Publishers, Copyright, 1992.

ISBN: 978-1-6642-1976-2 (sc)
ISBN: 978-1-6642-1927-4 (hc)
ISBN: 978-1-6642-1929-8 (e)

Library of Congress Control Number: 2021902211

Print information available on the last page.

WestBow Press rev. date: 02/10/2021

This little book is dedicated to my husband of more than sixty years. His steadfast faith brought me to a real knowledge of Christ and His love for me.

LOVE STORY

My, oh my, how the years have flown.
The children came and now they've gone.
Some years were fat; others were lean.
Some were filled with joy; others were pain.
But through it all, you held my hand,
Dried my tears, and said, "I understand."
So here we are with life in view,
And my heart still sings, *I love you*.
Darling, if we could our vows redo,
Love of my life, I'd still choose you.
(Written on July 25, 1999, for my husband on our
fortieth wedding anniversary)

INTRODUCTION

I began working on a study of David's life more than forty years ago. It has become my life's work to share what I have learned from this "man after God's own heart" (1 Samuel 13:14). I am not a scholar, and I don't presume to teach great theological lessons. However, I am a child of God who has learned throughout my nearly eighty years of living that God is always faithful and that I can depend on Him in every circumstance of my life.

I am always encouraged and uplifted when I read the way that David responded to God's leadership and always praised Him, even in the most dangerous and difficult times in his life. The following meditation tells you who I am and why I am here.

MY SAVIOR LEADS ME ALL THE WAY

> Then Moses went up from the plains of Moab to Mount Nebo, to the top of Pisgah, which is across from Jericho. And the Lord showed him all the land of Gilead as far as Dan ... Then the Lord said to him, "This is the land of which I swore to give Abraham, Isaac, and Jacob, saying, I will give it to your descendants—" ... So Moses the servant of the Lord died there in the land of Moab, according to the word of the Lord. (Exodus 34:1, 4–5)

I am almost at the top of life's mountain. I still have a little way to go before I reach the summit. I have been climbing for almost eight decades, and I'm getting tired of the climb. But as I stand here almost at the top of the mountain, I look down into the valley where I began. I remember the beautiful, happy times at the foot of the mountain when I was a child, growing up in a warm and loving family: four siblings, aunts, uncles, and cousins all around me. It was a wonderful time full of laughter and happiness.

Then I began the climb up life's mountain, wondering how long it would take and what I would have to endure to reach the top. The climb began with marriage to my high school sweetheart and the birth of three babies in less than three years. We struggled financially. Those were the bills, babies, and bologna years. Most of the time, they were filled with laughter, joy, and lots of love. Oh, there were difficult days when we struggled with financial and physical problems and school issues, but for the most part, it was a happy and wonderful time.

Then I reached the middle part of the mountain: an empty nest and then grandchildren. Those years were also filled with much love and laughter mingled with sadness and heartache when our first grandchild was born deaf and with Down syndrome. It takes a while to accept the reality that a child will always be dependent on others for the majority of her care.

But that sadness disappeared as she grew into one of the most loving and accepting people that I have ever known. She taught us what God's love was like: accepting and loving all people, regardless of the skin color, social standing, or economic status. She just loved them as God loves us.

But there were times when the climb was very difficult. There was no easy path to make my way joyful. There were dark times and sad days when death came—to my and my husband's parents and all those wonderful aunts and uncles. Then my husband's older brother, Paul, died. Recently, one of his younger brothers Jim died. They were times of unspeakable sorrow.

But here I am almost at the top. Like Moses, the Promised Land is not far away. I can almost see it from here. There's just a little more to go, and I will be at the summit. I would not change my position if I could. I do not want to go back, for you see, this journey is almost over for me. But along the way, I have learned some very important things about myself and the God that I have served for most of my life.

The blind hymn writer Fannie Crosby said it best when she wrote,

All the way my Savior leads me, what have I to ask beside?

Can I doubt His tender mercy who through life has been my guide?

Heavenly peace, divinest comfort, here by faith in Him I dwell

For I know what're befall me, Jesus doeth all things well.

All the way my Savior leads me, cheers each winding path I tread,

Gives me grace for every trial, Feeds me with the living bread.

Tho' my weary steps may falter, and my soul a'thirst may be,

Gushing from the rock before me, lo a spring of joy I see.

All the way my Savior leads me, O the fullness of His love!

Perfect rest to me is promised in my Father's house above.

When my spirit clothed immortal, wings it flight to realms of day

This my song through endless ages, Jesus led me all
the way.

My climb is almost over, and my life here is almost done. However,
I know that when this life is over, I shall stand in the very presence of
God. Revelation 21:4 declares, "And God will wipe away every tear
from their eyes; there shall be no more death, nor sorrow, nor crying.
There shall be no more pain, for the former things are wiped away." I
do not fear death; I look forward to that day when I will stand in God's
presence and experience His eternal blessing. Then I will sing through
endless ages, Jesus led me all the way.

I have structured this little book as a meditation and devotional
aid. I sincerely desire that you will find it useful day by day in helping
you to deepen your relationship to Christ.

DAY 1

But now your kingdom shall not continue. The Lord has sought for Himself a man after His own heart and the Lord has commanded him to be commander over His people, because you have not kept what the LORD commanded you.
—1 Samuel 13:14

The story of David begins with God's rejection of Saul in 1 Samuel 13:14. Samuel the prophet was speaking to Saul. Samuel said, "The Lord has sought for Himself a man after His own heart." This interaction between Saul and Samuel set in motion the events that would result in David eventually becoming king over Israel.

In 1 Samuel 16:1–13, we find the record of David's anointing. A familiar story begins in verse 1. God instructed Samuel how to find the new king. The passage says, "Fill your horn with oil, and go; I am sending you to Jesse, the Bethlehemite. For I have provided for Myself a king among his sons" (1 Samuel 16:1).

Samuel arrived in Bethlehem, and the elders in the town "trembled" at his presence. First Samuel 16:4 says, "The coming of God's prophet brought with it fear and apprehension of the town leaders, so they prepared a sacrifice for the townspeople and Jesse and his sons were invited to the sacrifice."

Eliab, the oldest of Jesse's sons, presented himself to Samuel. Samuel looked at him and thought,

> "Surely the Lord's anointed is before Him!" But the LORD said to Samuel, "do not look at his physical appearance" for man looks at the outward appearance, but the LORD looks at the heart. (1 Samuel 16:5, 7)

As each of the six remaining men passed before Samuel, God rejected them all. Samuel asked Jesse if he had another son, and Jesse replied, "There remains yet the youngest and … he is keeping the sheep" (1 Samuel 16:11). Samuel requested that David be summoned from his place of service and brought to him.

As David is brought before the prophet, God speaks again to Samuel and says, "Arise, and anoint him, for this is he" (1 Samuel 16:12). Samuel took the horn of oil and anointed him in the midst of his brothers, and 1 Samuel 16:13 says, "The Spirit of the Lord came upon David from that day forward."

The obvious conclusion from this episode at the beginning of David's story is that our choices are not God's choices. Samuel looked with favor on Eliab, and based only on his outstanding personal appearance (handsome and strong), he decided that Eliab was qualified to be king. It appeared to Samuel that he would be a capable king. He would be able to lead an army into battle and reign effectively. But God had another idea.

One by one, six more sons of Jesse were paraded before Samuel. One by one, God rejected each of them. In this large family of brothers, the youngest and least acceptable in the eyes of people was the one God chose.

This episode tells us clearly that God's standards are not ours. We look at people and like Samuel, judge them by external things, such as social standing, personal wealth, good looks, and prestigious occupations, while God looks at their hearts.

I recall an incident many years ago when my children were teenagers. We were on vacation when the church appointed a new student minister. After our vacation, I went to church and was very disappointed in the man that I saw. He wasn't handsome. In fact, he had hair down to his shoulders, and he didn't appear to be much older than my teens. I did not think that he had the appearance or experience to be the pastor that our church needed.

I began to pray that God would bring us a different person (one who would meet my expectations) or that that He would give me the ability to see what He saw in in the new minister. As I prayed over the situation, a transformation occurred. The transformation was not in the minister, but it was in me. I came to love that young man as a minister and a person. I learned to see him as God saw him.

Now some fifty years later, we still keep in touch. His life has been a blessing to me and many, many others. My prayer today is that God would give me eyes to see what He sees in people and that I would learn to know and love them just like He does.

Open my eyes, that I may see.
—Psalm 119:18

DAY 2

So he sent and brought him in. Now he was ruddy, with bright eyes, and good-looking. And the LORD said, "Arise and anoint him; for this is the one!" ... and the Spirit of the Lord came upon David from that day forward.
—2 Samuel 16:12–13

As the story continues, David did not refuse the anointing of the prophet because of his youth. He was not capable of being king over Israel at this point in his life, but he was willing to grow into a man who would be used by God. He was humble and willing to wait on the Lord.

Waiting on the Lord can be difficult. People who are called into God's service need to understand that their willingness does not necessarily equip them for the tasks that God has for them. David spent a long time in the service of Saul at his court. God was teaching him the skills that were necessary to reign as king. David's humbleness and willingness were two qualities that were very evident throughout his life.

Notice also that his anointing by Samuel was a private time of commitment between himself and God. Each individual must have a private anointing or salvation experience before beginning a life of service to the Lord.

From the day of his anointing, David was securely in the hand of God, even though he was not always in the will of God. He was marching toward a destiny that the Lord had planned for him. It would be many years before he was finally crowned as king over Israel, but when that days came, David established a capital city in Jerusalem. This event was recorded in 2 Samuel 5:9, which says, "Then David dwelt in the stronghold, and called it the City of David."

David's journey from tending sheep to becoming king took many years. He was thirty years old when he became king, and he ruled for forty years. All along the journey, he made mistakes that caused him much heartache. But David was consistent in his love for God, and he thanked Him for His watch and care over him. He was quick to express sorrow and to repent when he failed to be the man that God wanted and intended him to be.

This lifestyle is consistent with the way God expects all his anointed to live. Each of us has the anointing of the Holy Spirit, yet like David, none of us perfectly fulfills the will that God has for our lives. But like He was to David, God is faithful and just to forgive and restore us to fellowship and joy when we repent.

In Psalm 145:8, David writes, "The LORD is gracious and full of compassion. Slow to anger and great in mercy. The LORD is good to all, and His tender mercies are over all His works." He continues in Psalm 146:1–2, "Praise the Lord, O my soul! While I live, I will praise the Lord; I will sing praises to my God while I have my being."

In Romans 3:23, Paul writes, "For all have sinned and fall short of the Glory of God." But like David, we can repent and ask for forgiveness knowing that Jesus covered all our sins at Calvary and that God is still gracious and full of compassion. Psalm 145:8 tells us that He loves us just as we are: sinful, rebellious, self-seeking, and unworthy. He loves and forgives us anyway.

One of the lessons that we learn from this episode in David's life is that God still sees the person who is inside us, the one whose mind is focused on Him. Isaiah 26:3 says, "You will keep him in perfect peace whose mind is stayed on you." The word for *peace* in Hebrew is plural. It means *peace, peace*. God gives a double portion of peace to those who trust and depend on Him each day.

Even though David was a man of war who fought many battles, he wrote in Psalm 143:10, "Teach me to do your will, for You are my God." In the midst of the conflict, David's mind was focused on God, and he experienced that double portion of peace. My prayer today is that I have this perfect double portion of peace as I face the battles in my life.

DAY 3

And Saul's servants said to him, "surely a distressing spirit from God is distressing you ... now command your servants ... to seek out a man who is skillful in playing the harp" ... So Saul said to his servants, "Provide me now a man who can play well and bring him to me ... Then Saul sent to Jesse saying, "Please let David stand before me, for he has found favor in my sight."
—1 Samuel 16:14–23

The next major event in the life of David was his admission to King Saul's court. Had Saul known about David's anointing by the prophet Samuel, this event probably would not have happened. Saul would have recognized David as a threat to him and surely would not have allowed him to become part of his inner circle.

Saul was tormented with an evil spirit. The call was issued to find a musician who could soothe his troubled mind. One of the members of Saul's court recommended David, the son of Jesse and the Bethlehemite, as one who was "skillful in playing the harp" (1 Samuel 16:16). Saul commanded that he be brought to court. First Samuel 16:23 records, "And so it was, whenever the evil spirit was upon Saul, that David would take his harp and play. Then Saul would become refreshed and well, and the distressing spirit would depart from him."

David was brought to Saul's court so that he could learn. Even though Saul was not aware of David's status before the Lord, God had provided the opportunity for David to study at the feet of Saul. David was a mere shepherd boy, who was no doubt exceptional. But he still needed the polish and training that he would receive at king's court. David was in God's school, learning those things that would be necessary for him to know if he was to rule effectively and well when he became king.

God provided David every opportunity to develop the skills and knowledge that he would need so that he could perform well in battle and rule over Israel. He was a good student and used the opportunities that God gave him well.

This should be an example to us to pursue every opportunity to learn more about God's Word and His will for our lives. David was preparing to lead God's people, and the skills he was learning would be valuable throughout his life. God gives gifts to each of His followers. We need to develop those skills so that we can share about God's greatness with others.

Over and over again in the psalms, David declares the source of his strength and his joy. In Psalm 108:1–4, he says,

> O God, my heart is steadfast: I will bow down and give praise, even with my glory. Awake, lute and harp! I will awaken with the dawn. I will praise You, O Lord, among the people And I will sing praises to You among the nations, For Your mercy is great above the heavens, And Your truth reaches to the clouds.

This was written after David became king.

If we are to be witnesses to God's greatness and glory, we must learn as much as we can about Him and be able to declare His words to the people. In the psalms, we see the reason David is called a "man after God's own heart" (1 Samuel 13:14). He was not perfect. He committed sins that grieved the Holy Spirit, but he always repented, and God always granted forgiveness for those sins.

Today, I am praying that I will never stop studying and learning how to be the best I can be in my work and witness so that my life will have attributes that the One who saved me can use for His glory.

Not my will, but Thine be done.
—Luke 22:42

DAY 4

As he talked with them, there was the champion, the Philistine of Gath, Goliath by name ... and all the men of Israel, when they saw the man, fled from him and were dreadfully afraid ... Then David spoke to the men who stood by him saying, "Who is this uncircumcised Philistine that he should defy the armies of the living God?"
—1 Samuel 17:1–57

This story, which was recorded in 1 Samuel 17:1–57, is one that we all know well. It is the familiar record of David, the shepherd boy, defeating Goliath, the giant Philistine warrior. The story begins with David going to the battlefield with supplies for his brothers, who were serving in Saul's army. David was very young and not equipped to be a soldier.

However when he reached the battlefield, he found the Israelite army being defied by the Philistines. For forty days, the giant Goliath had been taunting the army and daring it to send someone to face him.

David asked the men who were standing beside him a question. In 1 Samuel 17:26, he says, "What shall be done for the man who kills this Philistine and takes away the reproach from Israel? For who is this uncircumcised Philistine, that he should defy the armies of the Living God?" David's eldest brother, Eliab, harshly rebuked David for leaving his sheep and coming to the battlefield.

David went to Saul and volunteered to face the giant. He said, "Let no man's heart fail because of him, your servant will go and fight this Philistine" (1 Samuel 17:32). He then told Saul of his success in killing both a lion and a bear and said, "And this uncircumcised Philistine will be like one of them" (1 Samuel 17:36).

Saul clothed David with his armor, gave him a shield, and put a helmet on his head. Young David fastened the sword to the armor, tried to walk, and then returned the armor to Saul. First Samuel 17:40 tells us, "He took his staff in his hand; and chose for himself five smooth stones from the brook and put them in the Shepherd's bag, a pouch which he had, and his sling was in his hand and he drew near to the Philistine."

David approached the giant, and the giant ridiculed him, saying, "Am I a dog, that you come to me with a stick?" (1 Samuel 17:43). David replies, "You come to me with a sword, a spear and a javelin. But I come to you in the name of the Lord of hosts … this day the LORD will deliver you into my hand" (1 Samuel 17:45–46).

We know how the giant ends in this tale. David takes one of the stones from his bag and hits the giant in the forehead. Goliath falls to the ground, and David kills him with his own sword. This familiar story leaves me with a question: Why did David need five stones when he was facing one giant?

We find the answer in 2 Samuel 21:16–22. The giants named in those scriptures were also sons of a giant who lived in Gath. Goliath had four brothers, who were Ishbi-Benob, Saph, Lahmi, and "a man of great stature who had six fingers on each hand … he was also born to the giant" (2 Samuel 21:20).

In those times, if someone killed a person, the dead person's family had the right and obligation to avenge the death of its relative. David was well aware of this cultural method of killing someone, so he was prepared to deal with any situation that he might encounter. He didn't know if he would confront one giant or five.

This is a marvelous message for us today. God promises victory to His people when they are prepared and they pray. He does not always tell us how great the battle may be. He expects us to go forth, be prepared for the worst, and trust Him to give us the victory.

God took a young inexperienced man and made him a great hero. He went in the strength of the Lord and faced an insurmountable problem with the assurance that with God at his side, he could be successful at defeating his foe.

It does not matter how many giants we face throughout our lives. Our giants may be physical, financial, or family problems—perhaps even death—but God has equipped us with everything we need to defeat them. It is wonderful to have the assurance that our God has already won the victory over all of life's giants. My prayer today is that like David, I can go forward with confidence and face life's giants with the assurance of victory.

DAY 5

Yet the Lord will command His loving-kindness in the daytime, and in the night his song shall be with me, and my prayer will be unto the God of my life.
—Psalm 42:8

The psalmist was aware of the presence of the Lord in every circumstance of his life. He honored God, revered Him, and called on Him in every situation. He thanked Him for each blessing, even during difficult situations.

God moves in our lives today and speaks to us just as clearly as He spoke to David. Too often, we think God doesn't speak to us, but in truth, God spoke, but we weren't listening. Like David, our hearts need to be tuned into Him. In order to hear the voice of God and to feel His hand touching us, we must look, listen, and diligently seek to know Him every day of our lives.

We look for instructions from God by studying His Word. His will for us is revealed by thoughtful study of the Bible. We will hear Him speaking to us from the pages of the Bible. He will reveal Himself to us as we study His word and diligently seek Him in prayer.

We also can see God's work as we observe natural phenomena. The psalmist recognized God as the Creator of all nature and acted upon that knowledge in seeking Him. We also can see God at work as we observe the touch of the Master's hand in our beautiful world.

Let us ask God today to make our hearts more in tune with Him so that we can see and hear Him in all the ways that He chooses to reveal Himself to us. Then let's thank Him for that revelation.

GOD CAME TO ME

God came to me one morning at daybreak.
In the sunrise, I saw His face.
He spoke to me as I met the morning
And gave me strength to greet the day.
God came to me at noontime.
As a small head bowed to say grace,
I thanked Him then for every blessing;
My home, my church, and my child's lovely face.
God came to me again in the evening,
When I was weary, tired, and worn.
He placed His loving arms around me.
He gave me rest, sweet rest, once more.
God came to me in afternoon,
In the power of a mighty storm.
He hurled the lightening across the sky,
As He hushed the maelstrom in my soul.
God came to me in darkest midnight,
Where no light could brightly shine.
He gave me joy in that dark hour.
Yes, I am His, and He is mine.
—Tommie McBrayer, 1980

DAY 6

Now it had happened as they were coming home, when
David was returning from the slaughter of the Philistines,
that the women had come out of all the cities of Israel,
singing and dancing … with tambourines, with joy, and
with musical instruments. So, the women sang "Saul has
slain his thousands and David his ten thousands."
—1 Samuel 18:6

In chapters 17 and 18 of 1 Samuel, we find David living at the palace
but also serving as a valiant soldier in Saul's army. He has gained a
reputation for being a great warrior.

The story continues with Saul becoming increasingly jealous of
David to the point of his trying to kill David. This is recorded in 1
Samuel 18:11, where it says, "And Saul cast the spear, for he said, 'I will
pin David to the wall.'"

Failing to kill David, Saul devised a scheme to have him killed in
battle. He made an offer to David. Saul would give David his daughter
in marriage. However, David would have to produce a dowry of one
hundred foreskins from the bodies of Philistine soldiers before the
marriage could take place. Saul made the offer thinking that David
would surely be killed in the effort to obtain the dowry.

Michal, Saul's daughter, loved David, and she was pleased that
this arrangement had been made. First Samuel 18:26 records, "And
it pleased David well to become the king's son-in-law." David was
successful in procuring the dowry requested by Saul.

First Samuel 18:28 records, "Thus Saul saw and knew that the
LORD was with David, and that Michal, Saul's daughter loved him.
And Saul was still more afraid of David. So, Saul became David's

enemy continually." This was the beginning of one of the darkest and most dangerous periods in David's life. He continually ran from Saul and knew that his life was in danger.

During this time of great stress and difficulty, David wrote some of his most beautiful psalms. In Psalm 56:3, he says, "Whenever I am afraid, I will trust in you." Psalm 57:11 says, "Be exalted, O God, above the heavens, Let Your glory be above all the earth."

Examples of David's unwavering faith are in every psalm, but none is more beautiful than Psalm 27:1, which says, "The LORD is my Light and my salvation; Whom shall I fear? The LORD is the strength of my life; of whom shall I be afraid." When David was afraid and could not see what lay ahead, he trusted in the Light to keep him safe.

Sometimes we experience situations where we cannot see or understand God's plan. But we can be assured that just like David, our Light will be sufficient to keep us safe and deliver us from the danger that we face. David recognized that Light. Jesus proclaimed to be that Light to the world, which drove away the darkness and fear. The last phrase of Psalm 23 expresses this concept so beautifully when it says, "Surely goodness and mercy shall follow me all the days of my life and I will dwell in the house of the LORD forever" (Psalm 23:6).

I was in a place that was dark and filled with fear. I could not see the way forward. In 1984, I wrote a hymn about that fear. The first stanza says,

> Sometimes the way is dark along life's pathway;
> I cannot see the way God planned for me.
> My heart is aching,
> My tears fall like raindrops,
> But still I'll praise His name for loving me.

Today I am asking God to remove all fear from my life and to bring that sweet peace that always comes when I am in the presence of the Light of the World.

DAY 7

Then David fled from Naioth in Ramah, and went to
Jonathan. "What have I done? What is my iniquity, and
what is my sin before your father, that he seeks my life?"
—1 Samuel 20:1

In 1 Samuel 19–20, we find David in great trouble. He went to Saul's
son, who was his friend Jonathan, and asked the question, "What
have I done? What is my guilt? And what is my sin before your father
that he seeks my life?" (1 Samuel 20:1). David's intentions toward Saul
were always pure and honest. He had not sought to overthrow the king.
He had only worked to serve him. He was intensely loyal to Saul, even
though Saul was determined to kill him.

Fleeing for his life, David ran to the prophet Samuel at the sanctuary
at Naioth. Samuel provided a place of safety for him in God's house.

So many episodes in David's life relate to our experiences today.
We see repeatedly in the psalms that he called on God when he was
in trouble. Psalm 124:7 says, "My soul has escaped as a bird from the
snare of the fowlers … and we have escaped." Psalm 120:1 says, "In my
distress I cried to the Lord and He heard me." There are many, many
other references to David calling on the Lord when he was in trouble,
but in Psalm 122:1, he said, "I was glad when they said unto me, let us
go into the house of the Lord."

Where did David go when he was having major problems and
could not see a way forward? He went to the prophet Samuel and to the
Lord's house. Too often, when things aren't going smoothly, we go to
our friends for advice or hurry to some outside source for counsel and
instruction. We become anxious and worry, asking, "What should I
do?" Our first stop should be at our place of worship, and our counsel

should come from our pastor. In Galatians 6:2, Paul tells us that we are to "bear one another's burdens." We will find comfort and help in God's house and with God's people.

In this great national crisis, we are staying at home and trying to be safe, but I know that we will rejoice as David did when all this is over. We will say, "I was glad when they said unto me, let us go into the house of the Lord" (Psalm 122:1).

Today I am rejoicing in my salvation and in the One who provided that salvation. He is the One who will see us through this pandemic and restore our land!

DAY 8

What have I done? What is my sin?
—1 Samuel 19:20

I have found no fault in him.
—1 Samuel 29:3; Luke 23:4

I want to revisit the scripture in 1 Samuel 19:20 when David asked the question, "What have I done? What is my sin?" The Bible has the answer. It tells us that God does not remember our sins and that they have been cast "as far away as the east is from the west" (Psalm 103:12).

In 1 Samuel 29, we find David being sheltered from Saul by the Philistine King Achish. David, along with his followers, had been helping the Philistine army in its battles with the surrounding tribes. The leaders of the Philistine army went to king Achish and complained that they were unhappy with David. They were afraid that he would try to overthrow the king and destroy them. King Achish listened to their complaint and told them in 1 Samuel 29:3, "I find no fault in him."

Read the passage where Jesus appears before Pilate, the governor and judge in Judea. He listens to the complaints of the Pharisees, washes his hands, and says, "I find no fault in him," (Luke 23:4). Psalm 103:12 declares, "As far as the east from the west, so far He removes our transgressions from us." Isaiah 43:25 says, "I will remember your sin no more."

In 1 Samuel 29, we clearly see David as a type of Christ in the Old Testament. Through David, God is giving us a glimpse of Jesus. Both men appeared before a ruler and a judge who had the responsibility of determining whether punishment was necessary because of some sin or indiscretion. They then would need to mete out punishment for that sin. The question, "What is my sin?" was answered by both Achish and Pilate using the exact wording, which says, "I find no fault in him" (1 Samuel 29:3; Luke 23:4).

When the time comes for us to stand before our King and Judge and the question is asked, "What is my sin?" we know from many scriptures that the answer will be, "I find no fault in him." God has promised us that our sin has been forgiven completely and forever. He sees us in the righteousness that was provided by Christ at Calvary.

John 3:16 is perhaps the best description of what God has given to us. John writes, "For God so loved the world that He gave His only begotten son that whosoever believes in Him shall not perish, but have everlasting life." From the Old Testament, Solomon writes in Ecclesiastes 3:14, "I know that whatsoever God does, it shall be forever … God does it that men should fear before Him."

We know that we receive salvation by grace through faith in Jesus Christ. His death on the cross paid the price for our sins. He received the punishment that we deserved on that terrible day. We also know that He came forth from the grave to give us eternal life and that He is living today.

Our salvation is secure, and our eternal destination has been determined by that question and incomparable answer. Jesus has paid the price for us and given us absolute assurance that we are His. Nothing can change our status or remove us from that position of grace. I am so thankful that He extended that grace to me.

Someday, I will stand before a King and Judge to ask the question, "What sin have I done?" His answer will be, "I find no fault in her."

DAY 9

This is the day the LORD has made; I will rejoice and be glad in it.

—Psalm 118:24

We do not know what was happening in the psalmist's life when he penned this beautiful psalm. We do know that he made a choice to rejoice and be glad.

Much of our lives are about the choices that we make, regardless of our circumstances. We may find that it is difficult to rejoice when we are weathering one of life's storms. It may be hard to see a cause for rejoicing in the midst of physical pain. Health issues that have no easy cure or ready remedy make it difficult to rejoice.

Perhaps the pain is not physical but is emotional, resulting from the loss of a loved one or difficult circumstances within the family. Perhaps financial pressures and job situations make it hard to see a way forward and through to a better future. Perhaps the issues are with children and/or schools.

Our lives are so complicated and difficult that sometimes we cannot see the proverbial light at the end of the tunnel. Yet the psalmist says, "This is the day the LORD has made, I will rejoice and be glad in it" (Psalm 118:24). The word *will* indicates an intentional action on the part of the writer, which culminates in joy. We can have joy in the midst of life's challenges and be glad in spite of them.

Sometimes the difficult days come to make us stronger and more dependent upon God's keeping power to see us through. Some of life's greatest blessings come because of struggle and difficulty.

One of those struggles came to me through the birth of a disabled grandchild. When she was born, I could see nothing good about the problem. How could this beautiful and sweet child's lifelong disability be something good? However, her life has become a source of great blessing. In her disability, she has taught me what God's love is like. This child has never shown enmity, prejudice, or disfavor to any person. She loves everybody equally. In her world, every person is worthy of love and treated with respect, regardless of their social standing, skin color, or gender. She just loves them and greets them with a hug.

Love is a choice, and when we learn to love others as God loves us, we will choose to rejoice! This is the day that the Lord has made. *I will rejoice* and be glad in it as I walk in sweet communion with the One who made the day.

DAY 10

David ... departed from there and escaped to the cave of Adullum. So, when his brothers and all in his father's house heard of it, they went down there to him. And everyone who was in distress, everyone who was in debt, and everyone who was discontented gathered to him. So, he became captain over them ... And there were with him about four hundred men.

—1 Samuel 22:1–2

I n the passage above, we return to Saul's persecution of David and find David living in a cave. David's life was in grave danger. He went to Moab to plead with the king of Mizpah. He requested to be allowed to bring his family to the cave while he waited on God to guide him. David's family joined him, and then others began to come, until a large number of people were following David.

This is a graphic picture of Christ and the Church. Like David, Jesus was in grave danger. He had to be tried in several different courts and executed before He could establish His church. Remember His poignant dying words from the cross when He said, "My God, my God, why have you forsaken me?" (Matthew 27:46). Christ had to enter the camp of the enemy, die, and then leave that camp victorious, in order to establish a new camp—a place where He could begin amassing his army, the Church.

Notice the kind of people who came to David. No one was worthy. They were poor examples of humanity. They were poor, discontented, and in distress. They were pictures of every sinner who comes to Christ. No one who is worthy comes to Jesus. Isaiah 64:6 tells us that our righteousness is as "filthy rags" in his sight. It is only as we come in repentance, realize our unworthiness and lack of ability to save ourselves, and ask for His grace that we can be saved.

They came to David seeking one who could offer them peace and safety and deliver them from their troubles. People come to Christ knowing that through Him alone, they can receive salvation from their sins and experience God's amazing peace.

The people came to David in every condition, and David turned no one away. John 3:16 tells us, "God so loved the world that He gave His only Son that whosoever believes in Him should have eternal life." Whosoever means anyone and everyone. God loves and forgives us just as we are. Then He transforms us into the "new creature" that Paul described in 2 Corinthians 5:17. We are made worthy because we are made worthy in Christ.

We see that the ones who came to David stayed to serve with Him. Christ saved each of us for a purpose and told us in Matthew 28:19 that our task was to "go into all the world and make disciples." Just as the followers of David had roles to play and jobs to do, we do as well. No one has an exemption from service. We all have spiritual gifts for service and power, through the Holy Spirit, to use those gifts.

David took this ragtag group of misfits and malcontents and turned them into the mightiest army his world had ever seen. Our David, Jesus, has built His church with the poor, lame, blind, destitute, unworthy, and unwanted, and it has grown into the most magnificent organization the world has ever known! I am so thankful that He included me and gave me a role to play in this glorious task.

DAY 11

I shall have joy in Your strength, O Lord, and in Your salvation, how greatly shall I rejoice!

> You have given me my heart's desire and have not withheld the request of my lips. For You meet me with the blessings of goodness. You set a crown of pure gold upon my head. I asked life from You, and You gave it to me—length of days forever and ever. My glory is great in Your salvation. Honor and majesty, You have placed upon me. For You have made me most blessed forever. You have made me exceedingly glad with Your presence. For I trust in the Lord. Through the mercy of the Most High, I shall be saved. … Be exalted, O Lord, in Your own strength. I will sing of Your power and praise Your name forever!
> —Psalm 21:1–7, 13 (paraphrased by Tommie McBrayer)

David wrote many psalms while he was in great danger. They proclaimed his dependence on God when he was beset by trouble on every side. This one, however, seems to have been written when he was in a period of great calm and a time of peace with men and the God who loved, protected, and saved Him.

It gives me great comfort to know that the same God loves, protects, and saves me. How can it be that He should look down on the billions of people that He created and choose one insignificant and little-known person to lavish His great blessings upon? I have often asked myself that question.

I was born the daughter of a coal miner. I am from an insignificant coal-mining community in the Appalachian foothills of northern

Alabama. Yet today, I am a child of the King of the universe. He has withheld no blessing, and He only asks that I serve Him with humility and that I be faithful to worship Him alone.

Look at my paraphrase of Psalm 21. In verse 1, He gives me joy. In verse 2, He answers prayer. In verse 3, He makes me a royal child. In verse 4, He promises eternal life. In verse 5, salvation is granted, and I am made worthy of honor. In verse 6, He promises eternal blessings in His presence. In verse 7, these blessings are granted through His mercy and not because I am worthy. In verse 13, it is because of His strength that I can sing and praise Him forever!

The little girl from the coal-mining community is a child of the King. Every blessing of my life is because of my trust in Him. He truly is the Way, the Truth, and the Life. He holds me in his hands. I still do not understand how He could save and love me, but I am convinced that He did and He does. Praise His name forever and forever!

Paraphrasing a scripture is simply saying it in your own words. It's a helpful tool that I use to personalize scripture. This is another version of my paraphrase of Psalm 21:1–7, 13.

(1) I shall have joy in Your strength, O Lord, and in Your salvation, I shall greatly rejoice.

(2) You have given me my heart's desire and have not withheld the request of my lips.

(3) You meet me with the blessing of Your goodness. You have set Your crown upon my head.

(4) I asked life from You, and You gave it to me. My length of days shall be everlasting.

(5) My glory is in Your great salvation, honor, and majesty that You have declared for me.

(6) For You have blessed me forever. You make me exceedingly glad in Your presence.

(7) I trust in the Lord, Most High, and through His mercy, I shall not be moved.

(13)   I will exalt You, O Lord, and I will sing and praise Your
name forever.

HE LOVES ME

He loves me. I am thankful.
He gives me joy unspeakable. I am thankful.
He knows my name. I am thankful.
He is my Savior. I am thankful.
He is Jesus. I am thankful.
—Tommie McBrayer, 2013

DAY 12

My God, My God, why have you forsaken me? Why are You
so far from helping me … I am poured out like water, and
all my bones are out of joint; My heart is like wax and it has
melted within Me. My strength is dried up like a potsherd;
My tongue clings to My jaws; You have brought Me to the
dust of death.

—Psalm 22:1–2, 14–15

Psalms 22, 23, and 24 are known as the Messianic Trilogy or the
Shepherd Psalms. They are all written by David. They present
Jesus in three different ways from three different perspectives.

As the Messianic Trilogy, they are prophetic, giving us a glimpse
of the past, present, and future. As the Shepherd's Psalms, they show
us who Jesus is. He is the Good Shepherd, who lays down His life for
the sheep. He is the Great Shepherd, who guides, guards, protects, and
provides for the welfare of the sheep. He is the Greatest Shepherd, who
is coming again to take His sheep to live with Him.

Addressing both of those perspectives, I want to look at Psalm 22,
one of David's most magnificent psalms. In Acts 2:29–30, Luke tells
us that David was a prophet.

Men and brethren, let me speak freely to you of the
patriarch David … being a prophet and knowing that
God had with an oath to him [David] that of the
fruit of his body, … He would raise up Christ … and
because he was a prophet he looked ahead and saw the
suffering of Christ on the cross.

David described that event in graphic detail one thousand years before it happened. This psalm reads as if David were standing at the foot of the cross and describing the event as it unfolded.

In the trilogy, we see a picture of the Good Shepherd who gives His life to save his flock. In 1 Samuel 17:37, David told King Saul that he had faced a lion and a bear to protect his sheep and that God had delivered him from danger. In the New Testament, Matthew 18:11–14, Jesus said,

> If a man has a hundred sheep and one of them goes astray, does he not leave the ninety-nine and if he should find it, I say to you, he rejoices more over that sheep than over the ninety-nine that did not go astray. Even so, it is the will of the Father who is in heaven that none of the little ones should perish.

Looking at today's psalm from both perspectives, we see a suffering Messiah who came to the world, was rejected by His own people, and died a horrible death. This event is in the past. It happened, and it was recorded by those who witnessed the event. It was also recorded by Josephus, the Jewish historian.

From the other perspective, in this psalm, we see the Good Shepherd who lays down His life for His sheep. Just as the shepherd in Matthew 18 was willing to face great danger and endure any difficulty to find that one lost sheep, so our Good Shepherd went to the cross in order to bring us salvation. Each one of us was that lost sheep that needed a Savior.

Today's psalm begins with the words of Jesus on the cross. The story ends with, "It is finished" (John 19:30). What was finished? The incomparable finished work of the Good Shepherd was salvation for His flock. I am humbled by and grateful to this Good Shepherd who died for me and brought me into His flock.

DAY 13

The Lord is my shepherd; I shall not want … and I shall
dwell in the house of the Lord forever.
—Psalm 23:1, 6

Psalm 23 is probably the most famous of all the psalms. It begins,
"The Lord is my shepherd; I shall not want" (Psalm 23:1). It is the
favorite psalm of millions of believers and quoted by many who are not
believers. Poetically, it is one of the most beautiful of all the psalms.

It begins with His promise to be with us always and everywhere
we go and to protect us from all evil. It ends with the promise of our
eternal security with Him. This psalm speaks to us in the present.
These promises are for us now and in this world with all its difficulties
and problems. It is a promise that God will never forsake us, just like
the Great Shepherd never left his sheep.

Several years ago while studying this psalm, I did a paraphrase
expressing what it meant to me. I am including it in this study. Perhaps
you will want to try paraphrasing to express your own thoughts about
the psalm.

PSALM 23

Lord, because you are my Shepherd,
I have everything that I need.
All that I want is to be more like you.

Your grace abounds in me,
According to Your riches in glory.
I rest in the green meadows of Your love.

You have made me one of Your anointed
And have protected me from the one
Who would destroy my soul.

You have provided for my every need
And have prepared a place for me
In your presence for eternity.
I am blessed.
(Paraphrased by Tommie McBrayer)

This wonderful psalm is like a beautiful gem in a crown. The others shine, and they are treasured, but this one is the brightest. Without it, the crown would be incomplete. It gives us a brilliant, bright, and wonderful picture of the Great Shepherd. I am in His flock. Are you?

DAY 14

The earth is the LORD's and all its fullness. The world and all those who dwell therein … Who may ascend into the hill of the LORD? Or who may stand in His holy place? He who has clean hands and a pure heart … Who is this King of Glory? The LORD strong and mighty … The LORD of hosts. He is the King of Glory.
—Psalm 24:1–4, 8, 10

Psalm 24 completes the trilogy. It presents Christ as the Greatest Shepherd. Sometimes He is called the Chief Shepherd, and it refers to future events. This great psalm begins with a declaration of who God is and ends with a promise that He will return.

In this Psalm, the Greatest Shepherd rewards His flock. It begins by reminding us that God created this earth and all that is in it. He gave it to Adam and Eve as a blessing. When they rebelled and sinned against Him, he removed them from their place of blessing. We have lived in that place of exile from His presence ever since.

However, His Word is filled with promises of the things that He has reserved for His people. John 14:1 says,

> Let not your heart be troubled, you believe in God, believe also in Me. In my Father's house are many mansions (dwelling places) and I go to prepare a place for you. And if I go, I will surely come again and receive you unto Myself, that where I am, there you may be also.

Revelation 7:17 says, "For the Lamb who is in the midst of the throne will shepherd them and lead them to living fountains of waters. And God will wipe away every tear from their eyes." In Revelation 19:16, He is called "KING OF KINGS AND LORD OF LORDS." Following that declaration, the judgment begins. The Book of Life is opened, and everyone is judged by whether or not his or her name is in that book.

In these three psalms, David gives us a complete and beautiful picture of Christ. In Psalm 22, He is the suffering Messiah, who died on a cross, and the Good Shepherd, who laid down his life for his sheep. We know that He came, He lived a sinless life, He died on the cross, and He was resurrected from the dead on the third day.

In Psalm 23, He is the Great Shepherd who takes care of his flock, protects them from harm, and provides everything that they need. In Psalm 24, He is the Greatest Shepherd, the Coming King, Lord of lords, and King of kings, who will come someday to reward His own with eternal life with Him.

Revelation 22:12–14 says,

> And behold, I am coming quickly, and My reward is with Me … I am the alpha and the Omega, the Beginning and the End, the First and the Last. Blessed are those who do His commandments, that they may have the right to the tree of life and may enter through the gates into that city.

I am looking forward to entering that city where I shall be forever with my Lord!

DAY 15

David inquired of the LORD saying, "Shall I go and attack these Philistines?" And the LORD said, "Go, attack the Philistines and save Keilah."
—1 Samuel 23:1

First Samuel 23 begins with David, once again, fleeing from Saul. His life is in danger, and Saul is relentless in his pursuit of him and his men. Saul has slaughtered the priests at the city of Nob in his pursuit of David. When David learns about the death of the priests and the family members of Abiathar, who was the only survivor of the massacre, David tells him, "Stay with me; do not fear. For he who seeks my life seeks your life, but with me you shall be safe" (1 Samuel 22:24).

We see in this chapter how relentless Satan is when he attacks the people of God and anyone associated with them. Saul had the priests killed in the attempt to get to David. However, faithful Abiathar went straight to the only one who could offer him a place of safety. He made no attempt to defend himself. He did not detour around David. He went to the place called "the Rock of Escape" (1 Samuel 22:28).

This is a difficult chapter because of the killing and persecution. This story tells us that Satan will be relentless in his pursuit of Christ and His Church. He seeks to destroy everyone who is loyal to Christ. In some cases, he will destroy their lives. We know there are many places today where Christians are openly persecuted and sometimes killed because of their faith. For others, he seeks to destroy their testimonies and witness for Christ. The only place of safety for us is our Rock, Jesus.

When David faced the incessant pursuit of his enemy, he went to the Lord for instruction and comfort. When we face the relentless pursuit of our enemy, we must do the same. Our only hope to escape the ravages of one who is determined to destroy our witness and perhaps take our lives is in that Rock of Escape, Christ.

David's words to Abiathar in 1 Samuel 22:23 were, "Stay with me, fear not." The word *stay* means *abide*. It indicates a state of continually being in the presence of the King. John 15:4–10 tells us that we are to "abide in Christ." The word *abide* is an active verb. Abiding in Christ is not a feeling or an emotion, but it is something that we choose to do. It means to remain or take a firm stand in our place. It entails far more than belief in the Savior. It is imperative that we exhibit a constant and consistent lifestyle that is rooted in our Rock of Escape. That is when we will be able to withstand the assault of Satan without fear.

First Peter 5:8 tells us that Satan is a "roaring lion, seeking whom he may devour." Paul tells us in 1 Corinthians 15:58 to be "steadfast, immovable, always abounding in faith … knowing that your labor is not in vain." If we are to abide in Christ, it must be a lifetime commitment to the One whom we serve. We must know that He alone is worthy of our complete devotion.

My prayer is for strength for *this* day. I'm abiding in Him, who has promised me a place of safety in His presence forever.

DAY 16

Look, this day your eyes have seen that the Lord delivered you today into my hand ... I will not stretch out my hand against ... the Lord's anointed.
—2 Samuel 24:10

David's struggle with Saul continues in 1 Samuel 24:1–15. David and his men were hiding in a cave. In 1 Samuel 24:3, Saul entered the cave and was "attending to his needs," when David slipped up behind him and cut a corner off Saul's robe.

When Saul left the cave, David called out to him, "Look, this day your eyes have seen that the Lord delivered you today into my hand ... I will not stretch out my hand against ... the Lord's anointed" (1 Samuel 24:10–11). Upon learning that, David could have killed him but had shown mercy to him, Saul responded to David's mercy by requesting one thing from David: a covenant that when David became king, he would not destroy all of Saul's descendants. David made and kept that promise to Saul.

There are many covenants and promises in scripture. The first one is in Genesis 3:15. God says to Satan and promises to Eve that she will have a descendant who will destroy Satan. "He shall bruise your head, and you shall bruise His heel." This is a prophecy with a promise that Satan would try to destroy Christ but that Christ would eventually destroy him.

The next one is in Genesis 9:15. God says to Noah, "I set my rainbow in the clouds and it shall be for a sign of the covenant between Me and the earth ... the waters shall never again destroy all flesh." In Genesis 12:2, God promises Abraham, "I will make you a great nation ... and you shall be a blessing."

There are many promises recorded in scripture. David says,

You bless the righteous, O LORD ... You cover them with favor. (Psalm 5:12)

He shall set me high upon a Rock. (Psalm 27:5)

When my father and mother forsake me, the LORD will take care of me. Psalm 27:10

Wait on the Lord, be of good courage and He shall strengthen your heart. (Psalm 27:14)

Weeping may last through the night, but joy comes in the morning. (Psalm 30:5)

Your unfailing love will last forever. Your faithfulness is as enduring as the heavens. (Psalm 89:2)

In John 14:1–3, Jesus made a promise when He said, "Let not your heart be troubled, you believe in God believe also in me ... I go to prepare a place for you, and if I go, I will surely come again that where I am, there you may be also."

The last promise in the Bible is in Revelation 22:12. Jesus tells John, "And behold, I am coming quickly, and My reward is with Me, to give to every one according to his work. I am the Alpha and the Omega, the Beginning and the End, the First and the Last." John concludes the passage in Revelation with, "Blessed are those who do His commandments, that they may have the right to the tree of life, and may enter through the gates into the city" (Revelation 22:14).

David understood the eternal nature of God. He had absolute assurance that God would keep His promises. He wrote in Psalm 25:14, "The secret of the LORD is with those who trust Him. And He will show them His covenant (promise)."

However, no matter how wonderful these promises and many others are, our faith is not rooted in the promises of God. *It is rooted in the One who made the promises.* Today, I am praising God, for He is a promise-keeping Savior!

DAY 17

And David said to Saul: "why do you listen to the words of men who say, 'Indeed David seeks to do you harm?' Look, this day the LORD delivered you into my hand … and I said 'I will not stretch out my hand against the Lord's anointed.'"

I Samuel 24:6

Perhaps more than any other, this passage shows us the reason that David was called the man after God's own heart. He was loving and merciful. He extended grace and offered forgiveness when justice required the death of Saul and the elimination of all his descendants.

Our David, Jesus Christ, has done the same thing for us. He has forgiven and forgotten all our sins. But is it possible for us to do something so egregious that God would take away that forgiveness? The answer is a resounding, "No!" The Bible promises us that everyone who comes to Christ in faith and believes will be saved. We are guilty, and we deserve to be punished, yet Christ died to make atonement for our sins. David extended mercy to Saul, and Christ does the same things for us.

There are many references in the Bible on this topic. But the best reason I know that I am eternally saved is that I was there when it happened! I clearly remember the event that changed me from a creature that was doomed to eternal death and separation from God to an instantly transformed child of God. Nothing can remove that memory from my mind.

But scripture also confirms that event. In John 10:27–30, Jesus says, "My sheep hear my voice and I know them … I give unto them eternal life and they shall never perish, neither shall any man pluck them out of my hand."

In Romans 8:38–39, Paul tells us, "That neither death nor life, nor angels, nor powers, nor things present nor things to come, nor height, nor depth, nor any other created thing, shall be able to separate us from the love of God, which is in Christ Jesus, our Lord."

Second Timothy 1:12 continues the thought with, "Nevertheless, I am not ashamed of the gospel of Christ, for I know Whom I have believed, and am persuaded that He is able to keep that which I have committed unto Him against that day." He is the one who keeps us from falling away, and we are not.

Another reason I know that I am eternally saved is the new nature that has come as a result of my salvation. John 1:12 says, "As many as received Him, to them He gave the right to become children of God, to those who believe in His name." We are children of the father. We are not perfect, and we sometimes disappoint Him, but we are still His children.

Finally, Ephesians 2:8 says, "For by grace are you saved through faith, that not of yourselves, it is the gift of God" I have been saved by the power of God and through the sacrifice that Jesus made at Calvary. I had no power to save myself. It came from God. My promise-keeping God has promised to keep me saved.

I thank God that the same grace through faith that saved me is the same grace that will keep me firmly in His hand throughout my life. I couldn't save myself, and I cannot keep myself saved. Praise God for His saving and keeping grace!

DAY 18

So, David said to the young man who told him "How did the matter go? Please tell me." And he answered, "The people have fled from the battle, many of the people are fallen and dead, and Saul and Jonathan are dead also."
—2 Samuel 1:4

Second Samuel begins a new chapter in David's life. Saul, who has persecuted him continuously for many years, is dead, and David is ready to begin his reign as king. David preceded this event with prayer. Second Samuel 2:1 records David asking the Lord, "'Shall I go up to any of the cities of Judah?' and God replied 'Go up ... to Hebron.'" Second Samuel 2:4 records, "Then the men of Judah came and there they anointed David king over the house of Judah."

David began his reign with prayer. Prayer was an integral and very important part of his life. The psalms are filled with instances of this great king asking for guidance and forgiveness when he sinned. It is also replete with psalms of praise and thanksgiving.

Jesus was also a man of prayer. Many times in the New Testament, we are told of His going away to be alone with the Father. He prayed for forty days in the wilderness when He was tempted. He prayed at the tomb of Lazarus. His prayer in the garden of Gethsemane, "Not my will but thine be done"(Luke 22:42) is poignant and moving. His words from the cross were a prayer: "Father, forgive them for they know not what they do" (Luke 23:34).

If it was necessary for David, the man after God's own heart, to pray, and if it was necessary for Christ, who had no sins to confess, to pray, how much more necessary is it for us to seek the Lord in prayer? There are several steps to deepening our prayer life.

David used his prayer time to confess and repent of his sin. Psalm 51:7–12, which he wrote after his great sin with Bathsheba, is the best example of this. He prayed,

> Wash me, and I shall be whiter than snow. (Psalm 51:7)

> Create in me a clean heart, O God. (Psalm 51:10)

> Restore to me the joy of Your salvation. (Psalm 51:12)

When we pray, confession must be our first priority.

David "inquired of the Lord" again in 1 Samuel 30:8, indicating that he was diligent and persistent in his prayer for guidance as he was preparing to become king. Jesus said in Matthew 7:7, "You have not because you ask not." We need to be persistent in our prayers.

Other elements our prayer should contain are praise and thanksgiving. Psalm 48:1, 9–10 records David praying,

> Great is the Lord and greatly to be praised ... We have thought, O God, on Your lovingkindness. In the midst of Your temple, According to Your name, O God, so is Your praise to the ends of the earth ... For this is God, Our God forever and ever; He will be our guide even to death. (Psalm 48:9–10)

In Psalm 104:2, David says, "Bless the LORD O my soul, and forget not all His benefits." This psalm is filled with reasons to be thankful.

After we have diligently sought the Lord in prayer, confessed our sins, and praised Him with thankfulness for all He has done, we are ready to begin praying for others. At this point, we need to look at our prayer lists and pray specifically for the people on them. Jesus prayed for his disciples in John 17, and he made specific requests on their behalf in His great prayer. We need to be specific when we pray for others.

In John 17:11–24, Jesus prays,

> Keep those whom You have given Me … that they may have My joy … Keep them from the evil one … Sanctify them by your truth … I also pray for those who will believe in Me through their word … that they may be made perfect … and that the world may know that you have sent me … Father, I desire that they also whom You gave Me, may be with Me where I am, and that they may behold My glory … And I have declared to them Your name, and will declare it, that the love with which You have loved Me may be in them, and I in them. (John 17:11–24)

Jesus made these nine requests for His disciples on the way to the garden of Gethsemane. Even as He made His way to His arrest, trial, and crucifixion, He was praying for others.

After we have confessed our sin, spent some time in praise and thanksgiving, and prayed for others, we can focus on our own needs. Perhaps our prayer will end just as Jesus's did with, "Not my will, but Thine be done" (Luke 22:42). I am thankful today for the wonderful privilege of communion with a God who knows my name, has made me His child, and listens to my prayers!

DAY 19

David's ongoing troubles with Saul often left him troubled and weary. In Psalm 6, he says,

> "Have mercy on me, O LORD, for I am weak. Oh Lord, heal me, for my bones are troubled. My soul also is greatly troubled: But You, O LORD, how long? I am weary with my groaning; All night I make my bed swim: I drench my couch with my tears. (Psalm 6.2, 6)

We can clearly identify with David in his troubles. Most of us have experienced difficult health issues. We have problems with our families and other people, which are not easy to reconcile. Sometimes, it seems that there will be no end to our troubles and that nothing can ease our physical and emotional pain.

But David continues his prayer in Psalm 6:9 with, "The LORD heard my supplication; The LORD will receive my prayer." David was troubled and weary, but he never gave up on God's ability to bring him through those difficult times. We read in Psalm 9:9, "The LORD will be a refuge for the oppressed ... in times of trouble. And those who know Your name will put their trust in You; For You, LORD have not forsaken those who seek You" (Psalm 9:10).

I wrote the following poem during a very difficult time in my life. I hope that you will find it meaningful.

WEARY

I am so tired, Lord, that today,
I cannot hear Your voice,

But I know that You are still speaking to me.
I am so tired, Lord, that today,
I cannot see Your face,
But I know that You are still smiling at me.
I am so tired, Lord, that today,
I cannot feel Your presence,
But I know that You are still with me.
Thank You, Lord, for loving me,
Even during those times when
I don't feel your presence
Or see your face or hear your voice
Because it is then
That I need you most.
—Tommie McBrayer, 1983

DAY 20

The beauty of Israel is slain on the high places! How the mighty have fallen! … Saul and Jonathan were beloved and pleasant in their lives, and in their death, they were not divided. They were swifter than eagles. They were stronger than lions … O Daughters of Israel, weep over Saul.
—2 Samuel 1:19–27

The last chapter of 1 Samuel records the final battle between the armies of Saul and the armies of the Philistines. First Samuel 31:6 records, "So Saul, his three sons, his armorbearer and all his men died together that same day."

Three days after the battle, David learns of the death of his nemesis. You would think that David would rejoice when he learned that the man who had persecuted him for more than a decade was dead, but that was not the case. Second Samuel 1:17 says, "David lamented … over Saul and over Jonathan his son." Rather than rejoicing over the death of his enemy, David called for a month of mourning for him and penned the beautiful epitaph given above.

How is it possible that David could be so forgiving after all Saul had done? He was relentless in his pursuit and persecution of David, murdered the priests at the temple in Nob, attempted to kill David at court when he threw a javelin at him, and made many other attempts on his life.

Remember that David was a type of Christ—someone who showed us what Christ is like in the Old Testament. He was the "man after God's own heart" (1 Samuel 13:14). He knew how to forgive. In Psalm 103:12, he said, "As far as the east is from the west, so far has He removed our transgressions from us." David was not perfect, but he was forgiven. He chose to forgive Saul when he had every reason and opportunity to rejoice in his downfall.

The Bible has many verses on forgiveness. Ephesians 1:9 says, "In Him we have redemption through His blood, the forgiveness of sins, according to the riches of His grace" Isaiah 1:18 says, "Come now let us reason together, though your sins be as scarlet they shall be white as snow." Jesus said in Matthew 6:9, "And forgive us our trespasses as we also have forgiven those who trespass against us."

It is difficult for us to wrap our minds around the act of forgiveness when someone has wronged us or hurt someone that we love. Indeed, this may be the most difficult area for Christians. We often hear it said, "Well, I forgave him, but I just can't forget it." I can't forget either, but I have chosen to forgive. Sometimes, it requires decades to reach the point where we can forgive.

In order to forgive others, I have to remember that God, through Christ, has forgiven me, not because I am worthy of forgiveness and redemption but because He loves me. I also have to remember that He loves the ones who have wronged and hurt me just as much as He loves me. His grace is available to them just as it was for me.

Like other principles in worship and faith, forgiveness is a choice. When you choose to forgive as you have been forgiven, God finally brings peace. David exemplified that peace when he wrote in Psalm 103:1–4,

> Bless the LORD O my Soul, and all that is within me, bless His holy name. Bless the Lord, O my soul, and forget not all His benefits. Who forgives all your iniquities, Who heals all your diseases, Who redeems your life from destruction, Who crowns you with loving-kindness and tender mercies.

I'm like David. I'm not perfect but far, far from it. I am forgiven. I have chosen to forgive what I once thought was unforgiveable. "Bless the LORD O my soul."

DAY 21

God blessed them and said to them "Be fruitful and increase
in number. Fill the earth and subdue it."
—Genesis 1:28

The concept of a family unit is extremely important. This concept was introduced in the very beginning of time. We find Adam and Eve in the garden of Eden. God's plan for creation was for men and women to marry and have children. They were to become one in union through marriage. They and their children would become a family, which was the essential building block of a stable and prosperous society.

The importance of the family can be seen in the provisions of the Ten Commandments. Two of the commandments related to the family. The fifth commandment tells us, "Honor your father and mother" (Exodus 20:12). This was intended for the children's benefit. It provided for a cohesive family structure with discipline. It was also a format that children could learn from their parents and grandparents. The seventh commandment addressed fidelity in the marriage relationship. Exodus 20:14 says, "You shall not commit adultery." God set the standard for marriage and stability in the family.

Second Samuel 3:1–5 records the beginning of David's family. Six sons came from six different mothers. Scripture records two more wives, ten concubines, and many more children. God has never blessed polygamy. David would experience much pain because of his very difficult marriages and many children.

Part of the breakdown in our society today can be traced to the destruction of the traditional family. Fathers are important. Mothers are important. They each have unique roles to play in the upbringing of children.

David would eventually experience great heartache because of his very large family and the inevitable conflicts that it produced. Many people today are experiencing similar heartaches and pain because of conflict within their families. However, God has another plan.

Jesus also talked about a theological family. He said, "Whoever does the will of my Father in heaven is my brother and my sister and my mother" (Matthew 12: 50). Jesus was not saying that our biological family was not important. He was expanding the concept of family to include those who are one in the Lord through their relationship with Him.

The parallels are clear. When we are born physically, we become part of a physical family. When we are born again, we become part of a spiritual family. Paul says, "You are all sons of God through faith in Jesus Christ" (Galatians 3:26).

I thank God today for my wonderful theological family in Christ. Your notes and calls of encouragement have meant much to me.

DAY 22

S econd Samuel chapters 3–6 record some interesting events in David's story. Chapter 3:1 begins, "Now there was a long war between the house of Saul and the house of David. But David grew stronger and stronger, and the house of Saul weaker and weaker." The political ramifications of several of these events would be long lasting and of great importance when David finally became king over Israel. The death of Ishbosheth and the restoration of Mephibosheth are two of those events.

Second Samuel 5:5–12 records the death of Saul's son Ishbosheth, who was king over the ten tribes of Israel, and the coronation of David as king over all Israel. Ishbosheth was murdered in his bed by men who were loyal to David. They brought Ishbosheth's severed head to David, thinking he would reward them for their deed. However, upon learning what they had done, David had them executed. He subsequently had Ishbosheth buried with the honor that was befitting a son of Saul and a king of Israel. The elders of Israel recognized that David was the man whom God had appointed to rule over them. They came to Hebron and anointed David as their king.

David had waited so many years for this event. He had reigned over the southern kingdom, Judah, for seven years. Now he would finally become king over the entire nation. David had endured many difficult years because God had promised him that he would become king. No doubt, there were times when he was discouraged; however, he was patient as he waited on God to fulfill that promise.

We can see many things in the events of David's life that remind us of Christ. Just as David was not accepted by the majority of Israel's tribes when Saul died, Christ wasn't accepted by the majority of Jews when He came. Just as David struggled for many years to win his title as king over Israel, Christ, through His church, has been struggling for a long time to become the King of kings and the Lord of lords that is spoken of in the Revelation. Just as David thoroughly conquered his opposition in order to become king, Christ has fought Satan and defeated death in order to become our eternal king.

Just as the time came when all Israel bowed their knees to David, so the time is coming when "every knee shall bow and every tongue confess that Jesus Christ is Lord" (Isaiah 45:23; Philippians 2:10). Just as David waited patiently on the Lord to bring him to that final appointed day when he would be king, Christ waits until the day that the Father has appointed, and only the Father knows when that day will be.

It is impossible for me to read these events in David's life without drawing the conclusion that as a type of Christ in the Old Testament, David gave us a complete and perfect picture of Christ. Like David, we tend to become discouraged and wonder when God will fulfill His promise to restore the earth and deliver His people. Revelation tells us that He is coming *soon*. Soon is an indefinite period. Soon has already been two thousand years.

Revelation ends with John saying, "Even so, come quickly, Lord Jesus" (Revelation 22:20). I long for the day when He will come again.

DAY 23

Now David said, "Is there anyone who is left of the house of Saul, that I may show him kindness (grace) for Jonathan's sake?" … And Ziba said to the king "There is still a son of Jonathan who is lame in his feet …" Then King David sent and brought him out of the house of Machir.
—2 Samuel 9:1–13

This is a very interesting chapter. Mephibosheth was the son of Jonathan and the grandson of Saul. Most of the time when a new king was installed, every living relative of the old king was put to death. But David had made a covenant with Saul, which promised that David would not destroy Saul's name and lineage when he became king.

> "Therefore, swear now to me by the LORD that you
> will not cut off my descendants after me, and that you
> will not destroy my name from my father's house. So
> David swore to Saul. (1 Samuel 24:21–22)

When Saul and Jonathan were killed in a battle against the Philistines, Mephibosheth, who was five years old, was taken from the royal palace by a nursemaid. In her hurry to escape, the nursemaid dropped the boy, and both of his feet were injured so that he walked with a limp the rest of his life. At the time that David asked about the descendants of Saul, Mephibosheth was an adult who was living in exile and in fear of being executed by David, who had finally been made king in Jerusalem.

You can imagine the apprehension and fear Mephibosheth experienced when he learned that David, who was now king over all

Judah and Israel, had requested his presence at the throne of the king. This event is recorded in 2 Samuel 9: 8. Mephibosheth prostrates himself before the king and says, "What is your servant, that you should look upon such a dead dog as I?"

Following this initial meeting, Mephibosheth becomes part of David's family. Second Samuel 9:13 records, "So Mephibosheth dwelt in Jerusalem for he ate continually at the king's table And he was lame in both feet."

This very interesting story is important for many reasons. It is the story of David extending grace to someone who was expecting only death because he was so unworthy. Mephibosheth had nothing to offer the king. Because of his disability, he could never serve as a warrior. Because of his lineage, he had every reason to believe that he would be executed.

Imagine his joy when David told him, "Do not fear, for I will surely show you kindness (grace) for your father's sake and will restore to you all the land of your grandfather, Saul, and you shall eat at my table continually" (2 Samuel 9:7).

Every Christian is like Mephibosheth. We are unworthy of the grace that has been freely given to us. We all have an inheritance that has been redeemed for us. The Bible tells us that Jesus is the bread of life and that we may eat of that bread continually. Revelation 19:9 says, "Blessed are those who are called to the marriage supper of the Lamb," where we will feast with our Lord continually in the place that He has prepared for us.

None of us is worthy. We deserve to die. But God has redeemed us by grace through faith in His Son, Jesus Christ. We are part of that great number that John saw in heaven, who were praising God forever and ever and feasting at His table.

I first heard this old gospel hymn as a child, and its message and melody have remained with me all my life. It speaks of that table where we will dine with our King.

COME AND DINE

Jesus has a table spread
Where the saints of God are fed,
He invites His chosen people, "Come and dine,"
With His manna He doth feed
And supplies our every need
Oh, 'tis sweet to sup with Jesus all the time

The disciples came to land,
Thus obeying Christ's command.
For the Master called unto them, "Come and Dine"
There they found their heart's desire
Bread and fish upon the fire
Thus He satisfies the hungry every time.

Soon the lamb will take His bride
To be ever at his side.
All the hosts of heaven will assembled be;
Oh, 'twill be a glorious sight,
All the saints in spotless white;
And with Jesus they will feast eternally.

REFRAIN

"Come and dine" the Master calleth, "Come and dine."
You may feast at Jesus' table all the time;
He who fed the multitude, turned the water into wine,
To the hungry calleth now, "Come and dine."
—Charles Widmeyer, 1907

Jesus tells us that He is the bread of life. Like Mephibosheth, who was unworthy of the grace that was extended to him, we may feast, even now and in this life, of that wonderful bread of life. For eternity, we will sit at the table of the King.

DAY 24

I will praise you with my whole heart; Before the gods I will
sing praises to you. I will worship toward Your holy temple,
and praise your name ... in the day when I cried out, You
answered me, and made me bold with strength in my soul.
—Psalm 138:1–3

This psalm came at the end of David's writing and possibly at the
end of his life. This high and holy psalm allows us to see the "man
after God's own heart" in a very personal way.

Psalm 138:1–3 says, "I Will give thanks with my whole heart ...
I will bow down toward your holy temple ... In the day I called you
answered me." When David said that he "will give thanks with my
whole heart," he was referring to the very depths of his being and core
of his existence. It represented all that he was and inferred that nothing
else was worthy of this measure of devotion.

Then he said, "Before the gods I will sing praises to You" (Psalm
138:1). David was declaring his faithfulness to Yahweh before the idol
gods of the nations around him. He was honoring God alone. This
constituted brave discipleship because those who believed in false gods
often persecuted anyone who challenged their beliefs.

Then he continued, saying, "I will bow down before your holy
temple" (Psalm 138:2). To bow down shows immense respect for the
one you are bowing down to. At the time this psalm was written,
the temple had not been built. David was probably referring to the
tabernacle in which the ark of the covenant resided. Solomon, David's
son, would build the actual temple. However, David was showing his
great reverence to the God, who would someday make His abode in

that actual temple. Revelation tells us about the eternal temple of God, where we will all bow down and worship the Lord for eternity.

He said, "And praise your Name ... for you have magnified your Name and your Word above all" (Psalm 138:2). Here the word *Name* is equal to what the name represents: *Yahweh Himself.* Yahweh has exalted Himself and shown His glory through His creation. Psalm 19:1 declares, "The heavens declare the glory of God. The firmament shows his handiwork." David was crediting God with all of creation. God also had declared an ongoing relationship with Israel. Yahweh's works and His Word brought Him glory. David was giving Him thanks for His faithfulness and loving-kindness in all aspects his life.

The final passage in these verses says, "In the day that I cried out, you answered me. And made me bold with strength in my soul" (Psalm 138:3). Here David revealed the reason that he had composed this hymn of praise. He had prayed for help, and God had responded by giving him strength and empowering him to conquer his enemies. His thanks and reverence penetrated to the depths of David's soul.

David, the man after God's heart, was a man of thanksgiving and praise. He was a man of prayer and reverence. He was a man who loved the Lord with his whole heart and honored Him with his life. It is the desire of my heart to be like David. I want to be thankful. I want to be bold and consistent in my witness. Today, I want to be a person of prayer, and I always want to give God the glory, "For great is the glory of the Lord" (Psalm 138:5).

DAY 25

All the kings of the earth shall praise you, O Lord, Yes, they shall sing of the ways of the LORD, for great is the glory of the Lord. Though the LORD is on high, yet He regards the lowly; But the proud He knows from afar.
—Psalm 138:4–6

These three little verses are packed with wonderful information and instruction for God's people. The first two lines tell us about a time when all the kings of the earth will honor God. They will declare before the world that Yahweh is the only God.

In Isaiah 45:23, we find the statement, "Before Me every knee shall bow." Paul quoted this is in Philippians 2:10–11, where it says, "As surely as I live, every knee shall bow." In Revelation, we learn that those who would not bow their knees in this world will have no part in His kingdom in the life to come. Revelation 20:15 says, "If anyone's name was not found in the book of life, he was cast into a lake of fire."

David was sure that His God was the giver of eternal life. In His time, everyone, from the smallest to the greatest, would acknowledge that He was God. Psalm 138:4 tells us that these people *will* come to faith by hearing the Word of the Lord. They may not believe today, but when they stand before the King of the Ages, they *will* believe; however, then it will be too late.

Paul wrote in 2 Corinthians 6:2, "Behold, now is the accepted time; behold, now is the day of salvation." Now is the time for Christians to be bold in their witness, give hope to the hopeless, and share the eternal Word of God with the whole world. The souls of people everywhere are in the heart of God. That is why Jesus told us, "Go, ye into all the world and make disciples" (Matthew 28:19).

Psalm 138:5 continues with the declaration that these kings will sing praise to God and will acknowledge the greatness of His glory. Psalm 138:6 changes from describing the whole earth giving praise to and recognizing Yahweh as the eternal God to giving a description of His character. It says, "Though God is high … he looks after the lowly, but the proud, He knows from afar" (Psalm 138:6).

The prophet Malachi describes what will happen to the *proud* in that day. Malachi 1:4 begins, "For behold the day is coming, burning like an oven, and all the proud, yes, all those who do wickedly will be stubble."

Revelation 20:14–15 tells us about the Day of Judgement, when this eternal punishment will be meted out. Those who have rejected the Living Word of God will be cast into the Lake of Fire: "Then Death and Hades were cast into the lake of fire. This is the second death. And anyone not found written in the book of Life was cast into the lake of fire" (Revelation 20:14-15).

In 2 Samuel 22:28 David wrote, "You will save the afflicted people, but your eyes are on the haughty that you may bring them down." This statement is repeated in Psalm 18:27, which tells us that God is interested in His people and that everything we have has been given to us by God. God has given gifts to each of His people, and He is always observing how we use those gifts and abilities.

Our gifts come in different forms. No two of us are exactly alike when it comes to the ways that we serve Him. However, the first and best gift that was given to the unworthy and afflicted people was the gift of salvation, which was accessed by faith through grace and given to us at Calvary. We all would be so afflicted without this incomparable gift. Nothing we have done or will ever do can compare to what God has already done for us through His Son, Jesus Christ. God and deserves all the glory.

DAY 26

Though I walk in the midst of trouble, You will revive me;
You will stretch out Your hand against the wrath of my
enemies, and Your right Hand will save me. The LORD
will perfect that which concerns me; Your mercy, O LORD,
endures forever; Do not forsake the works of Your hands.
—Psalm 138:7–8

The use of the term *right hand* is crucial to understanding this passage. Many times, the Bible uses the right hand to describe an important event.

Genesis 48:13 records the blessing of Israel on Joseph's sons, Ephraim and Manasseh, shortly before his death. Genesis 48:17–19 says,

> Now when Joseph saw that his father laid his right
> hand on the head of Ephraim, it displeased him …
> And Joseph said to his father, "Not so, my father,
> for this one is the first born; put your right hand his
> head." But his father refused and said I know, my son,
> I know. … he shall be great, but truly his younger
> brother shall be greater than he."

The right hand conveyed a great spiritual blessing.

In addition, when a person of high rank had someone at his right hand, it conveyed honor and recognized that the individual possessed equal authority with himself. Paul writes about Christ being seated at God's right hand in Ephesians 2:6: "And He seated Him at His right hand in the heavenlies."

David's use of the term, "Your right Hand will save me," is a messianic prophecy referring to one who has equal authority and power with God. The fact that Jesus is at the "right hand of God" (John 16:7–15) was a sign to the disciples that Jesus was indeed the Messiah. We can say, therefore, that God's right hand refers to the Messiah, whom we know as the Lord Jesus Christ.

Notice that Psalm 138:7 says, "Your right Hand will save." Acts 4:12 says, "Nor is there salvation in any there, for there is no other name under heaven … by which we must be saved." David and Paul recognized the importance of that right hand.

In Psalm 138:8, David told us that God would perfect or fulfill His purpose in the lives of those who follow him. He assured us of the eternal nature of God's mercy and grace. He also prayed for God's continuing faithfulness in guiding him. He said, "Do not forsake the work of your Hand" (Psalm 138.8). David was not expressing that he was uncertain that God's salvation was eternal. He was praying the prayer that we all pray. He was asking for God's continuing guidance in his life, knowing that without God's guidance, he would surely miss the mark of being the "man after God's own heart." This important psalm affirms the importance of the verses that declare that Jesus is sitting at the right hand of the Father.

Revelation 5:12–13 records John's vision of the throne room in heaven. He says,

> And I saw in the right hand of Him who sat on the throne a scroll … and I looked and behold, in the midst of the throne … stood a Lamb as though it had been slain … then He came and took the scroll out of the right hand of Him who sat on the throne … and they sang a new song, saying: "You are worthy to take the scroll, and to open its seals. For you were slain and have redeemed us to God by your blood. Out of every tribe and nation and tongue … and have made us kings and priests to our God and we shall reign on the earth … Worthy is the Lamb who was slain …

blessing and honor and glory and power to Him who
sits on the throne and to the Lamb, forever and ever.

This passage concludes with, "Then the four living creatures said.
'Amen!' … And … the elders fell down and worshipped Him who lives
forever and ever" (Revelation 5:14).

Even so, come quickly, Lord Jesus!
—Revelation 22:20

DAY 27

O LORD, You have searched me and known me. You know
my sitting down and my rising up. You understand my
thought afar off. You comprehend my path and my lying
down, and you are acquainted with all my ways. For there
is not a word on my tongue, but behold, O Lord, you know
it altogether. You have hedged me behind and before, and
laid Your hand upon me. Such knowledge is too wonderful
for me. It is high, I cannot attain it.
—Psalm 139:1–6

Omniscience is the state of having total knowledge, the quality of
knowing everything, without the processes of thought, reason
or inference. In the first six verses of this psalm, David declares that
God is omniscient. Psalm 139:1 begins, "You have searched me and
known me."

Acts 1:24 records the apostles' request for wisdom when choosing
a disciple to replace Judas. Joseph, called Barsabas, and Matthias were
being considered. The writer, Luke, records their prayer: "And they
prayed and said, You, O Lord, who knows the hearts of all, show which
of these You have chosen" (Acts 1:24). The apostles believed in the
omniscient nature of God.

Matthew 9:4 tells us Jesus knew the thoughts of His audience. "But
Jesus, knowing their thoughts, said, 'Why do you think evil in your
hearts? For which is easier, to say, Your sins are forgiven you, or to say,
Arise and walk?'"

Psalm 139:2–6 tells us that God knows everything about us. He
knows our "sitting down and rising up." This indicates that God is
aware of all our activities, twenty-four hours a day. Waking or sleeping,

he knows when we are working, playing, or sleeping. He is concerned about our daily activities.

David said, "You are acquainted with all my ways, for there is not a word on my tongue. But behold, O LORD, You know it all together" (Psalm 139:4). He knows what we are going to say before we say it. Isaiah says, "It shall come to pass that before they call, I will answer; and while they are still speaking, I will hear" (Isaiah 65:24).

He knows your routine, every thought, and everything there is to know about you. He knows you better than you know yourself! God knows His people completely. He knows all the evil ways of His people, and He is aware of every good deed. He knows where your heart is at and how genuine your faith is.

Psalm 139:5 tells us that our omniscient God has created a hedge or safe path for us to walk on. David had a very close relationship with Him, and God was guarding his way and clearing the path.

Psalm 139 continues in verse 6 as David described His knowledge as "too wonderful" and "high" and declared that he could not attain it for himself. In Psalm 131:1, David said, "LORD, my heart is not haughty, Nor my eyes lofty. Neither do I concern myself with great matters, nor with things too profound (difficult) for me." This acknowledged that he, David, did not have the same kind of knowledge that God had.

Our God is the creator of everything. He knows everything about us, from our "rising up and sitting down" (Palm 139:2). Every aspect of our lives is known by Him. Jesus said, "I and my Father are one" (John 10:30). We can be confident that our Redeemer is aware of every need that we have in every moment of every day. He alone knows the depths of our beings and sees the contents of our hearts.

There is an old hymn that was written by Edwin Orr in 1918, which says,

> Search me O God, and know my heart today.
> Try me O Savior, know my thoughts, I pray.
> See if there be, some wicked way in me.
> Cleanse me from every sin and set me free.

I praise you Lord, for cleansing me from sin;
Fulfill Your Word and make me pure within.
Fill me with fire, where once I burned with shame,
Grant my desire Lord, to magnify your name.

Only an omniscient God can be our Savior and cleanse us from sin. Jesus said, "I am the way, the truth and the life. No one comes to the Father except through me" (John 14:6).

First Corinthians 14:12 says, "Now I know in part, but then I shall know as I am known." Someday we will have great knowledge. The God who saved us will show us how great our sin was so that we can understand the magnitude of the grace that saved us.

I am thankful for an omniscient Savior who is, even now, sitting at the right hand of the Father and preparing a place for me in His presence.

DAY 28

Where can I go from your Spirit? Or where can I flee from your presence? If I ascend into heaven, You are there; If I make my bed in hell, behold You are there. If I take the winds of the morning, And dwell in the uttermost parts of the sea, Even there Your hand shall lead me, and Your right hand shall hold me. If I say, Surely the darkness shall fall on me, Even the night shall be light about me. Indeed, the darkness shall not hide from You, but the night shines as the day. The darkness and the light are both alike to You.
—Psalm 139:7–12

In the first six verses of this psalm, David talked about the omniscience of God. In these verses, he is discussing the omnipresence of God. He is telling us that God is everywhere at all times. We can never go to a place where He cannot find us. What a comforting thought that is! Because He is a watchful Father, His children are never far from Him.

Notice that Psalm 139:7 says, "Where can I go from Your Spirit? Or where can I flee from Your presence?" David believed in the indwelling and empowering Spirit of God. Psalm 143:10 says, "Teach me to do Your will, For You are my God: Your Spirit is good. Lead me in the land of uprightness." Psalm 51:10 and 12 also mention, "Your Holy Spirit." Who is the Holy Spirit that David knew and revered?

The doctrine of the Trinity tells us much about Him. In John 16:5–7, Jesus gave us a promise that after His death, He would send a helper who would come and convict the world of sin. That promise is fulfilled in Acts 2:1–4. Luke records, "When the Day of Pentecost had fully come … there came a sound from Heaven, as a mighty, rushing wind … and they were all filled with the Spirit." That day changed everything for the disciples. They were transformed from men who had been cowering in fear for fifty days to evangelists who transformed the world with the gospel all because of the empowering that they had received from the Holy Spirit.

Who is this Holy Spirit? The Holy Spirit is a person, and He has many qualities. I will list some of them for you here:

> He speaks. (Revelation 2:7; Acts 13:2)
> He intercedes. (Romans 8:26)
> He testifies. (John 15:26)
> He leads. (Acts 8:29)
> He commands. (Acts 16:6–7)
> He guides. (John 16:13)
> He appoints. (Acts 20:28)
> He can be lied to. (Acts 5:3 4)
> He can be insulted. (Hebrews 10:29)
> He can be grieved. (Ephesians 4:30)
> He can be blasphemed. (Matthew 12:31–32)
> He is eternal. (Hebrews 9:14)
> He is all-powerful. (Luke 1:35)
> He is omnipresent. (Psalm 139:7)
> He is omniscient. (1 Corinthians 2:10–11)
> He is called God. (Acts 5:3–4)
> He was present at creation. (Genesis 1:2)

He was the divine inspiration for the written Word of God. The Bible tells us, "Holy men of God spoke as they were moved by the Spirit of God" (2 Peter 1:21).

Psalm 139:8 has a confusing phrase. It says, "If I ascend into heaven, You are there; if I make my bed in hell, You are there." The word *hell* means the abode of the dead or the grave. Even after we die, God is there. We can be sure that God will never forsake His people and that His unfailing love will be with us even as we walk through the "valley of the shadow of death" (Psalm 23:4).

The psalmist continues and refers to the "wings of the morning" and the "uttermost parts of the sea" in Psalm 139:9. This is a reference to immense distances. We can never go to a place where God cannot go. He continues this thought in Psalm 139:10. He says, "Even there Your hand shall lead me and Your right hand shall hold me." No matter where the people of God go, He will be there, leading them like children, providing for their needs and comfort, and giving them peace.

David continues in Psalm 139:11–12, saying, "If I say, Surely the darkness shall fall on me", Even the night shall be light about me, Indeed the darkness shall not hide from You, But the night shines as the day. The darkness and the light are both alike to You." The darkness cannot prevail against the light, and light always prevails over darkness. What a comfort it is to know that even in the darkest nights of our souls, God is there and He will take away the darkness with the light of His presence and the knowledge of His love for us.

David's great faith is evident in these verses. He was secure in knowing that God was everywhere, all the time, and at the same time. He (David) could never be separated from His presence, even in the hardest, most difficult times of his life. The same God that was with David is with us today. He is the eternal God who never changes, and He is the one who knows us better than we know ourselves. He is always protecting His children and providing for their welfare.

Just as David believed in the omniscience of God, he also believed in the Holy Spirit and God's omnipresence. We serve a mighty God and have a wonderful Savior, but we also have the *helper* that Jesus promised to send to us. He will never leave us or forsake His own.

DAY 29

For You formed my inward parts; You covered me in my mother's womb. I will praise You, for I am fearfully and wonderfully made. Marvelous are Your works, and that my Soul knows very well. My frame was not hidden from You. When I was made in secret and skillfully wrought in the lowest parts of the earth. Your eyes saw my substance being yet unformed. And in Your book, they were all written. The days fashioned for me, when as yet there were none of them. How precious also are Your thoughts, O God, How great is the sum of them! If I could count them, they would be more in number than the sand. When I awake I am still with You.
—Psalm 139:13–18

The word *omnipotent* means *all-powerful*. There is no greater passage of scripture to discuss the power of an omnipotent God than this one. God's omnipotence is seen in every aspect of His creation. God said, "Let there be" (Genesis 1:1–31), and the heavens, the earth, and all its creatures came into existence. Psalm 33:5–7 tells us, "By the word of the LORD were the heavens made ... He gathers the waters of the sea together ... Let all the earth fear the LORD, let all inhabitants stand in awe of Him."

However, in Psalm 139:13–16, we see how God divinely engineers and protects an unborn child. The God who loved, cared for, and protected us while we were unborn continues protecting, guiding, and loving us throughout our lives.

God's power is also seen in the way He has preserved the things that He created. All life as we know it would cease to exist, if not for the all-powerful creator sustaining and maintaining everything that He created.

> For by Him all things were created that are in heaven and in earth ... and in Him all things consist. (Colossians 1:15–16)

God's power extends to human governments and leaders. In Daniel 2:21, we see where scripture records a vision that Daniel had. He responds to God by saying, "Blessed be the name of God forever. For wisdom and might are His. He changes the times and the seasons; He removes kings and raises up kings." In John 19:11, Jesus says to Pilate, "You could have no power at all against Me unless it has been given to you."

Politics are very divisive today. People with strong and opposite opinions dominate the newscasts and radio shows. There is much division in our land because of the increasingly loud opinions on each side. But we need to remember Daniel 2:21: "He removes kings and raises them up." The changes in our political leaders will be determined by God. He alone knows when and how those changes will occur. We may fret and complain, but God alone has the ability to do something to end the conflicts and create peace in our land!

Scripture tell us that Jesus is also omnipotent. We see His power throughout the New Testament in the miracles that He performed. Matthew 14:16–21 records the feeding of the five thousand with just five loaves and two fish. Matthew 8:24 records the calming of the sea. Matthew 11:18–28 records His raising a girl from the dead and healing a blind man. There are many other miracles recorded in Matthew, as well as in other parts of the New Testament. Only an omnipotent God could do all these things.

Because God is omnipotent, He cannot do things that are contrary to His holy character. For instance, Numbers 23:19, Titus 1:2, and Hebrews 6:18 teach us that God cannot lie. Lying is contrary to His holy character.

In spite of hating evil, God allows it to happen. He made people with free will. Even though He has the power to stop it, He allows it to happen. Paul says in Romans 8:27–28,

> Now He who searches the hearts knows what the mind of the Spirit is, because He makes intercession for the saints according to the will of God. And we know that all things work together for good to those who love God, to those called according to His purpose.

As long as we are in this world, God will allow evil to continue, but in awe, we continue to look for the city that is not made with hands, where we will be free from all evil.

In Psalm 139:17–18, David expressed his amazement at the infinite mind of God and compared it with the limited minds of men. He wrote, "How precious also are Your thoughts to me, O God! How great is the sum of them!" David was convinced that the God who created Him was the God who also provided for His salvation. We know that salvation was provided at Calvary through the death of Jesus Christ, who was God Incarnate, living with His people and then dying for them.

As God Incarnate, Jesus Christ is also omnipotent. His power is seen in the miracles He performed, the sinless life that He lived, but ultimately in His resurrection from the dead. Death is the ultimate reason that Jesus came—He came to destroy death! He stated this clearly in John 2:19: "Destroy this temple, and in three days I will raise it up." The Jews thought that He was talking about Solomon's temple. They did not understand that He was speaking about the *temple* of His body. He had the power to call legions of angels to rescue Him, but instead, He gave Himself to be the ultimate, final offering that would take away the sins of the world.

DAY 30

Oh, that You would slay the wicked, O God. Depart from me, therefore, you bloodthirsty men. For they speak against You wickedly; Your enemies take Your name in vain. Do I not hate them, O LORD, who hate You? And do I not loathe those who rise up against You? I hate them with perfect hatred. I count them my enemies. Search me, O God, and know my heart; Try me, and know my anxieties. See if there is any wicked way in me, and lead me in the way everlasting.

—Psalm 139:19–24

In Psalm 139:19–22, David was venting his feelings toward the ungodly people in the pagan nations around him, but he did not question the authority of God to deal with unbelievers as He saw fit. He maintained his faith in a gracious and loving God, even when he couldn't understand the reasons that God did not act.

He did not understand the reason why his enemies and those who did not respect and honor God were allowed to continue in their wicked ways. He was confused and troubled, but he never questioned God's faithfulness toward those who followed him. Psalm 139:19–20 describes people who were very wicked and bloodthirsty. David declared his hatred for them. He said that they were his enemies.

Isaiah spoke of a time when God would act with finality on this problem. He wrote,

> With righteousness He shall judge the poor, and decide with equity for the meek of the earth. He shall strike the earth with the rod of His mouth, and

with the breath of his lips, He shall slay the wicked. Righteousness shall be the belt of His loins, and faithfulness the belt of His waist. … For the earth shall be full of the knowledge of the LORD, as waters that cover the sea. (Isaiah 11:4–5, 9)

Isaiah is making a prophetic statement about the end time, when God will right all the wrongs that David was so concerned with.

In Psalm 139:22, David says, "I hate them with perfect hatred, I count them as my enemies." David is not neutral toward them and has no response to the enemies of God except hatred. He didn't hate *the people* who were committing the sins, but he hated *what the people were doing.* Hatred in this sense is not sin. It is sin to disregard and overlook people who are God's enemies.

Christians need to be consistent with David. We need to speak against the evils of our day, even if we cannot understand why God allows it to continue to grow. Scripture is very clear on the fate of Satan and his followers. Revelation 20:9–12 describes the fate of the wicked: "And fire came down from God out of heaven, and devoured them. The devil, who deceived them, was cast into the lake of fire and brimstone … And they will be tormented day and night forever and ever."

The final verses of Psalm 139 record David's obeisance, even when he could not understand God's purpose. The dictionary definition of *obeisance* is *deferential respect.* Without understanding the reason why, David believed that God was in control of his life and knew his heart's desire was to serve Him, even when he couldn't see or understand God's plan for eternity.

In Psalm 139:23–24, David asked God to search his heart and to find any wicked way in him. His final plea was, "Lead me in the way everlasting." Revelation gives us the answer to David's prayer. Revelation tells us, "And God will wipe away every tear from their eyes; there shall be no more death, nor sorrow nor crying. There shall be no more pain, for the former things are passed away" (Revelation 21:4–7).

David did not understand why God allowed evil to exist and

did not punish those responsible for that evil. He did not have God's complete revelation to help him understand, but he still had faith and trusted God to lead him in the way to everlasting life.

Isaiah expressed the solution to David's dilemma. He wrote, "You are my servant; I have chosen you and have not cast you away. Fear not, for I am with you; Be not dismayed for I am your God. I will strengthen you, Yes, I will help you, I will uphold you with My righteous Right hand" (Isaiah 41:10–11). When we cannot see the way before us and don't know the reason why, we must be like David and trust in God's unfailing love.

Revelation 21:6–7,24 tells us,

> And He said to me, it is done! I am the Alpha and the Omega, the Beginning and the End. I will give of the fountain of the water of life freely to him who thirsts. He who overcomes shall inherit all things. I will be his God and he shall be My son… And the nations of those who are saved shall walk in its light and the kings of the earth bring their glory and honor into it.

Finally from Isaiah again,

> I have sworn by Myself, the word has gone out of My mouth in righteousness and shall not return, that to Me every knee shall bow and every tongue shall take an oath and he shall say Surely in the LORD I have righteousness and strength. To Him men shall come, and all shall be ashamed who are incensed against Him. In the Lord all the descendants of Israel shall be justified and shall glory. (Isaiah 45:23–25)

In Jeremiah 31:3, the Lord tells the people through the prophet, "I have loved you with an unfailing love." I am thankful today for God's wonderful Word, which brings comfort, peace, and joy to my heart!

DAY 31

Then it happened one evening, that David arose from his
bed and walked on the roof of the king's house. And from
the roof he saw a woman bathing, and the woman was very
beautiful to behold. So, David sent and inquired about the
woman. And someone said, "Is this not Bathsheba ... the
wife of Uriah, the Hittite? Then David sent messengers, and
took her, and he lay with her.

—2 Samuel 11:2–5

This passage records the infamous story of David and Bathsheba.
You know the story well. The king was at home. Normally,
he would have been with his troops participating in the battle with
Israel's enemies. For some unknown reason, David had decided not to
participate in the fray.

From his rooftop, he saw a beautiful, young woman bathing.
David's rooftop would have been his patio. From that viewpoint, he
observed Bathsheba, who was probably in an enclosed garden area that
was not open to public view. He was smitten from that first view and
sent for her to come to the palace.

The Bible tells us about the visit and the pregnancy that resulted
from the visit. The pregnancy was reported to David, and he attempted
to bring Bathsheba's husband back from the battle to sleep with his
wife so that the liaison would be covered up. Uriah refused to go to
Bathsheba, preferring to stay with his troops.

When it became obvious that they could not cover up the sin,
David made matters worse by sending Uriah to the hottest part of
the battle, where he was killed. Following the death of Uriah, David

brought Bathsheba to the palace, made her one of seven other wives, and the child was born.

Nathan the prophet came to David. Nathan told him a parable about a rich man who took a prized sheep from a poor man and killed it, even though he had many sheep of his own. David became so angry about this story, which he believed to be true, he responded by saying, "As surely as the Lord lives, the man who did this must die! He must pay for that lamb four times over, because he did such a thing and had no pity" (2 Samuel 12:5–6). Then Nathan pointed to David and said, "You are the man" (2 Samuel 12:7)

Following the confrontation with Nathan, David composed Psalm 51. This is one of the most moving of all the psalms. In it, we see the broken heart of a man who has committed a great sin. It reads in part,

> Have mercy upon me, O God, according to the multitude of Your tender mercies. Blot out my transgressions, wash me thoroughly from my iniquity, and cleanse me from my sins … My sin is always before me, against You, you only, have I sinned and done this evil in Your sight … Purge me with hyssop, and I shall be clean; wash me and I shall be whiter than snow … hide your face from my sins and blot out all my iniquities … restore to me the joy of Your salvation and uphold me by Your generous Spirit … Deliver me from the guilt of bloodshed, O God, the God of my salvation and my tongue shall sing aloud of Your righteousness and my mouth shall show forth Your praise. (Psalm 51:1–14)

Psalm 32 reflects the attitude of David after God had forgiven him. It begins,

> Blessed is he whose transgression is forgiven; whose sin is covered. Blessed is the man to whom the LORD does not impute iniquity, and in whose Spirit there is

no deceit … I acknowledged my sin to You, and my
iniquity was not hidden and You forgave the iniquity
of my sin. (Psalm 32:1–5)

People need to know that there is no limit to God's forgiveness.
In Romans 5:20, Paul writes, "Where sin abounded, grace did much
more abound."

No one, not even the man after God's own heart, was perfect. But
he did suffer the consequences of his sin. The child born to him and
Bathsheba died. David suffered a loss of his reputation, and he lost the
joy of fellowship with God. Only when he repented did God restore
that joy. Notice that David did not say, "The joy of *my* salvation." He
knew that salvation came from God and that joy was the result of
God's salvation.

This account of David and Bathsheba teaches many lessons. First,
you cannot hide your sin from God. Second, God forgives anyone who
repents. Third, even after being forgiven, someone who sins will still
suffer consequences from that sin. Fourth, God can still accomplish His
purpose in the life of one who has committed egregious transgressions.

Romans 6:1–2 says, "What shall we say then? Shall we continue
in sin that grace may abound? Certainly not! How shall we who (have)
died to sin live any longer in it?" Romans 6:17 continues, saying, "But
God be thanked that though you were slaves of sin, yet you obeyed
from the heart … you were delivered and having been set free from sin,
you became slaves of righteousness."

David obeyed from his heart, confessed his sin, and God forgave
him of murder, adultery, covetousness, and lying. He is willing to
forgive us of so much more today.

DAY 32

So David said to Nathan, "I have sinned against the LORD" And Nathan said to David "The LORD also has put away your sin; you shall not die, However, because by this deed you have given great occasion to the enemies of the LORD to blaspheme, the child also who is born to you shall surely die" ... And the LORD struck the child ... and it became ill. ... Then on the seventh day it came to pass that the child died ... When David saw that his servants were whispering, he perceived that the was dead. ... So David arose from the ground, washed and anointed himself ... and He went into the house of the LORD and worshipped ... Then his servants said to him "What is this that you have done? You fasted and wept for the child while he was alive, but when he died you arose and ate food." David said "while the child was alive, I fasted and wept ... but now he is dead; why should I fast? Can I bring back again? I shall go to him, but he shall not return to me."
—2 Samuel 12:13–23

Weeping may endure for a night, but joy comes in the morning. (Psalm 30:5)

This sad passage tells a story that everyone can relate to. We have all lost people who were very dear to us. We remember them with great affection and look forward to a time when we shall see them again in heaven. David was sure that he would see his baby again.

When I think of this story, I also think of Paul's first letter to the Thessalonian church. He wrote,

> I do not want you to be ignorant, brethren, concerning those who have fallen asleep, lest you sorrow as others who have no hope. ... For the Lord Himself will descend from heaven with a shout, with the voice of the archangel, and with the trumpet of God. And the dead in Christ will rise first. (I Thessalonians 4:13–16)

Who are these others who have no hope? They are the persons who have never trusted Christ as their Savior. They do not believe that He was born of a virgin, He lived a perfect and sinless life, He died a vicarious death on the cross as a sacrifice for the sin of the world, He was buried, and He was raised again on the third day. They do not believe that He sits today at the right hand of God, the Father, and that He is coming soon to establish an eternal kingdom. Those people have no hope.

Rather than being hopeless, Hebrews 11:1 tells us, "Faith is the substance of things hoped for. The evidence of things not seen." Hope for the Christian is our absolute assurance that God is going to do what He said He would do.

What has He (Christ who is God and equal with the Holy Spirit and God, the Father) said that He would do? John says,

> Let not your heart be troubled, you believe in God, believe also in me. In My father's house are many mansions {another meaning for mansions is dwelling places}and I go to prepare a place for you. If I go and prepare a place for you, I will surely (most certainly or without doubt) come again and receive you unto myself, that where I am, there you may be also. (John 14:1–3)

That is what He said He would do. But can we be sure it will happen? According to Numbers 23:19, we can depend on His word: "God is not a man and He does not lie." We can be sure that Christ is coming again and that He has prepared a dwelling place for those who trust in Him.

That brings us to other questions. Who and what will be in our dwelling place? Is it possible to can take something with us to that eternal home? I believe we can. My mind goes to the Old Testament. In Jeremiah 31:3, God told Jeremiah to say to the people, "I have loved you with an everlasting love." I wondered if God's everlasting love could be compared to human love. Again, I believe it can.

I believe heaven is a wonderful place where we will experience God's everlasting love throughout eternity. I also believe our dwelling place is one, where for eternity, we will be with our family, our children, our spouse, and others that we have known and loved. We will enjoy God's love for us and experience a transcendent human love with those who have preceded us to heaven. I believe this transcendent human love, like God's love, is everlasting. It is higher, deeper, and broader in scope than anything we have experienced on earth. I believe we will share that great love throughout eternity in our dwelling place.

David had the hope that Paul wrote about. He believed that he would see his child again.

Now that brings me to my last question. Have you trusted Christ for your salvation? If you are not sure that you have made that decision, will you do it today? I want you to be there at my dwelling place so that we can experience God's love for us and our perfect love for each other throughout eternity.

For God so loved the world that He gave His only begotten son, that whosoever believes in Him shall not perish but have everlasting life.
—John 3:16

CONCLUSION

Let us hear the conclusion of the whole matter: Fear God and keep His commandments, for this is man's all. For God will bring every work into judgement, including every secret thing, whether good or evil.
—Ecclesiastes 12: 13–14

D avid's son, King Solomon, gives me the perfect verse to conclude this study of David's life. In the books of 1 and 2 Samuel, he was exposed for all to see. Several lessons that he learned from life are valuable for us today. I am revisiting some of the things that we have already learned from David. They are "the conclusion of the matter" (Ecclesiastes 12:13).

1. First, we saw that David had a personal relationship with God. When Samuel anointed David, he accepted the challenge that God had given him. David's relationship to God was established before he began his work. Each Christian must have a personal relationship with Christ. There is "no other name given under heaven whereby we must be saved" (Acts 4:12).

2. Second, we see David diligently preparing for the work that God had anointed him to do. He spent years in service to Saul, learning the things that were necessary for a king to know. All Christians have been called to serve. We must prepare carefully for the job that God has called each of us to do.

3. Third, David was intensely loyal to Saul, even when Saul was determined to kill him. David recognized Saul as the man whom God had allowed Samuel to anoint as Israel's king. Even

though Saul wanted him dead, David refused to participate in any attempts to destroy Saul. He said, "I will not raise my hand against the Lord's anointed" (2 Samuel 24:10). Scripture teaches us that God raises up kings and that He alone will remove them. Christians need to respect and honor our "king." God will remove him when it is time.

4. Then we saw David forgiving Saul when human nature would have had him mortally wounding Saul because of his persecution and hatred for David. Christians must have a forgiving spirit, even when we encounter situations that seem unforgiveable.

5. We also see that David was very courageous. He entered into battles that seemed to be overwhelming. He was constant in his battle, courageous in his position, and dependent on God for the victory. Christian soldiers today must be valiant and strong as we face the enemies of God. We may be certain that the ultimate victory is assured and that God will give the victory.

6. We also saw David fleeing to the house of God in times of trouble. He sought God at the place where He could be found. Perhaps more than at any other time in our history, today we need to be aware that there is a place of safety and refuge in Christ. Our confidence can be placed in the One who is able to deliver us from all the uncertainty and turmoil.

7. We looked at a period in David's life when he lost his victory and suffered sorely because of sin. This should be a warning to us never to become so secure in our own strength that we stop depending on the Lord. Just as David lost his joy and his relationship with the Lord was damaged, so we also can lose our joy and victory. Sin can damage our witness and destroy our fellowship with other believers and God.

8. After David committed the great sin with Bathsheba, we saw him return to God in repentance and sorrow for his sin. This characteristic is the one that really makes David one of the most outstanding role models in scripture. He was not perfect,

but when he sinned, he came back to God and asked for forgiveness and restoration. We saw how God responded to that repentance and restored fellowship and joy for David. When we sin, we can be sure that our God is "faithful and just to forgive all unrighteousness" (1 John 1:9).

9. David was generous in his praise of others. Upon learning of the death of Saul, David did not gloat or otherwise demean the fallen leader. Instead, he composed a beautiful epitaph to the man who had been Israel's first king. David had every reason to be glad that Saul was dead, yet he was filled with respect, and he praised him. Like David, we should look for something positive and good to say about others—even those who were not kind or just toward us.

10. We saw that David was patient. He was willing to wait for God to accomplish His will in himself. David did not get ahead of God and try to remove Saul. Sometimes it is difficult for us to "wait upon the Lord" (Isaiah 40:31). We want to go in our own strength, and that usually results in failure.

11. Then we looked at David as a man of prayer. He inquired of God and waited for an answer. If we would be like David, we must make prayer a priority. We must take time to offer praise to a Holy God. We must thank Him for His many blessings in our life. We must take all our needs and supplications to Him and listen for His answer. Most of the psalms are prayers.

12. We also saw in the scripture that David set goals for his life. He inquired of God, and when the answer came, he set about to accomplish the task put before him. Christians who serve effectively must have purpose in their serving. We cannot randomly choose to do a task and then suddenly change our minds. We must set goals for service that have purpose.

13. David knew the key to successful living. His life was surrendered to God, and because of that, God blessed him. To become successful in our service, we must be surrendered. We cannot keep a portion of our lives for ourselves. We must give it all to Jesus.

14. We saw that David suffered. Yes, he was successful, and yes, he had the key to abundant life, but God did not exempt him from the battle and pain. Christians will endure suffering and pain, but often, those situations are used by God to help us grow our trust and faith in Him. A mature Christian will be able to praise God and give Him the glory, even in suffering.

15. Finally, we saw that David was aware of his unworthiness to stand before a Holy God. Only through God's grace could he be redeemed. We must never depart from the truth that God's grace is our only sufficiency or the only righteousness that we can claim. Like David, we have one hope, and that is to trust in the redeeming power of Jesus Christ for our salvation.

For by grace are you saved through faith, and that is not of yourselves, it is the gift of God, not of works lest any man should boast. For we are His workmanship, created in Christ Jesus for good works, which God prepared beforehand that we should walk in them.
—Ephesians 2:8–10

POTPOURRI

This section is not related to the life and work of David, but has miscellaneous pieces I have written or material I have used in preparing for Bible study classes for many years. I hope you find it meaningful.

WISDOM FROM SOLOMON

For I know whatsoever God does, it shall be forever.
Nothing can be added to it and nothing taken from it.
God does it that men may fear (trust) him.
—Ecclesiastes 3:14

These words from Solomon, the richest man in the world of his day and the son of the great King David, remind us that everyone, no matter how rich or privileged, needs to know God. When David died and Solomon was made king, God told Solomon to ask for anything, and that desire would be granted. In 1 Kings 1:8, Solomon responded to God's inquiry, saying, "Therefore, give to Your servant an understanding heart to judge Your people, that I may discern between good and evil" (1 Kings 3:9). Solomon may not have known just how profound his request to God was, but the resulting wisdom from it has given us the wisdom book of Ecclesiastes.

Our verse for today says, "I know whatsoever God does; it shall be forever" (Ecclesiastes 3:14). God's Word is not temporary. His words and works endure forever. "Nothing can be added to it and nothing taken from it" (Ecclesiastes 3:14). We cannot improve on God's work or take away from it. It is eternal.

Then the third phrase in Ecclesiastes 3:14 says, "God does it, that men may fear (trust) him." That is a very profound thought. God gives wisdom to men who trust Him, and that wisdom is forever. Nothing we do with our human wisdom will improve what God has said. Nothing we can do can take away from it. Eternity was in God's control when He created humans, and love for the humans that He created was in His heart.

But the most important thing God gave us was his Son, Jesus Christ, as the propitiation for our sins. John 3:16 says it best: "For God so loved the world that he gave his only begotten son, that whosoever believes in Him shall have eternal life." Nothing can be added to it (no works of ours are needed), and nothing can be taken from it (If we take away the cross, there can be no redemption). God does it so that people may trust Him.

I trusted Him a long time ago. Have you?

THE PRAYER OF JABEZ

And Jabez called on the God of Israel saying, "Oh, that You would bless me indeed, and enlarge my territory, that Your hand would keep me from evil, that I may not cause pain!" So God granted him what he requested.

—1 Chronicles 4:9–10

J abez is a well-known character from scripture. His name means *pain*, indicating that his mother may have had a difficult time giving birth. Apart from that, we know nothing about his upbringing and family. However, based on this simple prayer, we know that he trusted God and that he faithfully followed Him.

There are five elements to the prayer of Jabez.

1. He requested God's blessing in his life.
2. He asked God to expand his territory.
3. He asked God to guide him in his everyday endeavors.
4. He asked for protection from harm.
5. He asked God to keep him from causing pain to others.

We all need those five elements in our lives.

In every prayer, we should ask God to bless us, our families, and those around us. We know God honors those prayers as we faithfully pray for the health, healing, and salvation of the people in our lives. We thank Him for that greatest of blessings, the gift of salvation, which came through the death, burial, and resurrection of His Son, Jesus Christ.

Second, he asked God to expand his territory or influence so that he could expand and grow. We need to expand our territory to include the people that we meet who need to know our Savior. Jesus told us that our territory was the whole world. He said, "Go into all the world and make disciples" (Matthew 28:19). Missions was in the heart of Jabez, and it surely is in the heart of Christians today. Our territory is still waiting to be expanded, as long as there are people who have not heard the gospel.

Third, Jabez asked God to guide him every day. That surely is one of our greatest needs. We need to be guided by the Holy Spirit so that we will not stray from the truth. Scripture tells us, "Satan is like a roaring lion, seeking those whom he may devour" (1 Peter 5:8). Satan cannot take away our salvation, but he is working every day to destroy our testimony and our fellowship with God.

Fourth, Jabez asked for protection from harm. Jesus asked for this same thing in His model prayer in Matthew. He said, "Deliver us from the evil one" (Matthew 6:13). We have a cohort of angels standing ready to protect and preserve us. That is their primary responsibility.

Fifth, Jabez did not want to cause pain to any other person. He asked God to help him in his relationships with other people so that he wouldn't cause pain, either physically or emotionally, to anyone in his family or sphere of influence. Oh, that is desperately needed in our world today. Christians need to be leaders in expressing our desires and feelings in ways that cause no pain.

James tells us in his letter that the "tongue is like a fire" (James 3:6) and that it can cause great damage if uncontrolled. We are also warned about gossip, which can destroy the reputation of a good person. The desire of our hearts should be to cause no pain. My dad taught me the saying, "If you can't say something good about someone, don't say anything at all."

Jabez's prayer is very relevant for us today. It reminds us of God's eternal blessing to those who trust in Him. It tells us that it is the responsibility of every believer to expand our territory and to be a witness of God's grace throughout the world. It reminds us that we do not have to work alone because we have a helper, the Holy Spirit, to guide us every day. It reminds us that it is okay to ask for God's help when we face temptation.

Lastly, it tells us to cherish our relationships so that we cause no harm or pain to any other individual. What a great message this is in such a little passage. I am glad that Jabez's prayer is included in our scripture.

THE NAME ABOVE ALL NAMES

> Therefore, God also has highly exalted Him and given Him
> the name which is above every name, that at the name of
> Jesus every knee should bow … and every tongue confess
> that Jesus Christ is Lord.
> —Philippians 2:9–11

When my husband and I named our children, we didn't give any thought to what the names meant. We chose names that we liked and that had some family significance, but we did not know the actual meaning of those names.

In the Bible, names have great significance. They were chosen carefully by parents to express some hope, dream, or perhaps revelation from God about the person's character or ability. It is interesting that Joshua is called *God is salvation*. Jesus is also called *God is salvation*. Joshua is the Hebrew name for Jesus, which in the Greek.

David's name means *commander*. Of course, He became the great commander and king of the Jewish people. Miriam means *bitterness*. Mary means *stubborn or obstinate*. Perhaps the mothers of these girls had difficulty with their pregnancies. Thus, the names described the hardship of their births.

The great apostle Paul was originally called Saul, which means *asked of God*. After his conversion on the road to Damascus, he became known as Paul, which meant *little*. Interesting that little Paul was a man of great humility, was one of the greatest apostles, and wrote more than a third of the New Testament.

We are linguistically challenged when we try to describe God, but it was not so for the writers of scripture. They used many beautiful and colorful words to describe God.

Elohim is frequently used in the Old Testament. It comes from two Hebrew words. The first, *El*, means *powerful,* and the second part, *him*, means mighty. We express it as great and mighty. This name for God is plural, therefore in Genesis 1:26, God says of Himself, "Let Us make man in Our image. Elohim is our great creator, assisted in creation by the Son and the Holy Spirit."

The most frequently used name for God is *Jehovah*. It is used more than 2,600 times in the Old Testament. God used this name to identify Himself to Moses at the burning bush. It is often used as *Yahweh*, which means *I am the God who has always been, who is, and who shall always be*. He is the Great I Am. He revealed Himself to Moses at the burning bush. He reveals Himself to us through His Son, Jesus Christ, who proclaimed, "I AM the way, the truth and the life, no one comes to the Father but through me" (John 14:6).

There are many, many other names used for God, but these two are sufficient for is to understand that no matter what name we use, He is the Eternal God who loved us enough to provide a way for us to be saved through his Son, Jesus. That salvation is secure because the One who saved us—the Great I Am—is also the one who keeps us.

Not of works, lest any man should boast. (Ephesians 2:9)

GUIDE ME, O THOU GREAT JEHOVAH

Guide me O Thou great Jehovah,
pilgrim through this barren land,
I am weak, but Thou art mighty,
hold me with Thy pow'rful hand;
Bread of Heaven, Bread of Heaven,
Feed me till I want no more,
Feed me till I want no more.

Open now the crystal fountain,
whence the healing waters flow,
Let the fire and cloudy pillar
Lead me all my journey through.
Strong Deliver'r, Strong Deliver'r
Be Thou still my strength and shield
Be Thou still my strength and shield.
—William Williams, lyrics and John Hughes, music

WONDERFUL PROMISES

Having therefore, these promises dearly beloved, let us
cleanse ourselves from all filthiness of the flesh and spirit,
perfecting holiness in the fear of God.
—2 Corinthians 7:1

The Bible is filled with wonderful promises from God. They leap
forth from its pages to bring joy and blessing to the child of God.
Therefore, how should we conduct our lives in light of God's goodness
to us?

Paul answers that question very clearly in his second letter to the
Corinthians. We are to cleanse ourselves from all unrighteousness
and strive always to project the image of Christ. We are to do so in
reverential awe of the God who created us and made a way for our
salvation.

We begin the process of cleansing with a daily bath in God's Word
and our confession of total unworthiness to Him. We cannot reflect
Christ to a lost and dying world if our lives are cluttered and marred
by sin. Christ is faithful and just to forgive us when we ask Him to.
In the Book of Hebrews, Chapter 8:12 the Bible says that For I will
be merciful to their unrighteousness, and their sins and their lawless
deeds I will remember no more." Today I am claiming the wonderful
promise of forgiveness from "all lawless deeds" so that I can live in a
way that honors Him.

WONDERFUL PROMISES

Wonderful promises God has given.
My grace will all thy need supply.
My strong arm will never fail thee,
and I will guide thee with Mine eye.

Wonderful promises God has given.
I will remember your sin no more.
I will come to take you with Me,
and you shall live forevermore.

Wonderful promises God has given.
Grace brings life that is full and free.
Not by works of my own merit,
Salvation is a gift to me.

Wonderful promises, wonderful promises
That are fulfilled in Christ upon the tree.
Living again, ascended to Heaven,
Coming tomorrow for you and me.

—Tommie McBrayer, 1979

STAND FIRM IN YOUR FAITH

Watch, stand fast in the faith, behave like men, be strong.
—1 Corinthians 16:13

Sometimes we become tired—physically and emotionally exhausted—and wonder how we can make it through another day. If our exhaustion occurs because of our service to God and His Church, we wonder if our effort is really worth it. During times like these, the Bible speaks clearly about the necessity of remaining firm in our stand for Christ.

We are not promised a life of ease while following in the footsteps of Jesus. To the contrary, Jesus warned us that we must be prepared to endure hardship and suffer sorrow. He also promised never to leave or forsake us during those dark hours.

The exhortation above was given to the Corinthian church during such a time of hardship and great stress. Paul was encouraging those Christians to place their feet firmly on the rock of faith, which is Christ Jesus, and then to stand.

The same principle is relevant today in a world that causes so much stress and difficulty. Christ is the same yesterday, today, and tomorrow. If we are to stand firmly in our faith, we must stand on Him. He is the Rock of our salvation, the Defender of our faith, and our Advocate before the Father. Through Him and Him alone, we can find the wisdom and strength that we need to overcome the world and all its temptations.

Stand fast in the faith ... be strong. We are more than conquerors through Christ!

GOD HAS NOT PROMISED

God has not promised skies always blue,
Flower strewn pathways all our lives through,
God has not promised sun without rain,
joy without sorrow, peace without pain,
God has not promised we shall not know,
trial and temptation, trouble and woe,
He has not told us we shall not bear,
many a burden, shed many a tear.
But God has promised strength for the day.
Rest from our labor, light for the way,
Grace for our trials, help from above,
Unfailing sympathy and undying love.
—Anonymous

THE VALLEY OF DECISION

Multitudes, multitudes in the valley of decision, for the day
of the Lord is near in the valley of decision.
—Joel 3:14

The prophet Joel speaks of a time when multitudes of people will
hear the voice of God, and they will be moved to make decisions
regarding their relationship with Him. Today, perhaps as in no other
time in history, people have the opportunity to hear the Word of the
Lord and respond to it. Media has allowed us to present the gospel in
ways and places that have been previously impossible. Christ has called
His people to service, which gives us an unprecedented opportunity
for Christian outreach. He has truly given us the means to reach the
multitudes for Him.

Perhaps you are one of those "multitudes in the valley," and you
have a decision to make. Is Christ calling you to a greater role and a
deeper commitment to service? Have you really made a decision to
serve Him with your whole heart? Sometimes God allows us to be "in
the valley" so that we can reflect on our lives and respond to His call.

Think about your life and the decisions that you need to make in
order to better serve God. Ask God to lead you out of that "valley of
decision" to a mountaintop of joy in serving Him. I wrote the following
poem in the 1970's when I was struggling with spiritual issues. It means
a lot to me.

IN THE VALLEY

Are you in the valley of decision?
Is your heart so full of strife
That you cannot see the Master,
And do not know His will for your life?

Multitudes are in the valley.
Their cares are endless; joys are few.
Sorrow is their chief companion,
Till Jesus comes to see them through.

Have you questions that need an answer?
Are you pained in heart and soul?
Are you tossed by storms unending,
Without an anchor for your soul?

Jesus is your only answer.
He can fill your every need.
Leave the valley of decision.
Follow the Lord where 'er He leads.
—Tommie McBrayer, 1979

SALVATION

For God so loved the world that He gave his only begotten
son that whosoever believes in Him should not perish but
have eternal life.

—John 3:16

The doctrine of salvation by grace through faith is the bedrock of
our faith. John 3:16 is probably one of the best-known verses in
the Bible.

Why do we need salvation? The Bible teaches us
All have sinned and come short of the Glory of God
(Romans 3:23)
All we like sheep have gone astray. (Isaiah 53:8)
There is none righteous, no not one. (Romans 3:10)
Salvation is not received by working for it.
It is not of works, lest any man should boast.
(Ephesians 2:9)

Paul stated in Philippians 3:5 that his works were greater than
his contemporaries were. He said, "I was a Pharisee of the Pharisees,"
but his zealous activity in the name of religion was not sufficient for
salvation. To the contrary, it separated him from God's grace.

If our works have no efficacy for salvation, how then can we be
saved? Nicodemus came to Jesus at night and asked, "What must I do
to be saved?" Jesus told him, "You must be born again" (John 3:1–21).

Isaiah points out man's problem. Isaiah 59:2 says, "Your iniquities
have separated you from your God; and your sins have hidden his face
from you so that He will not hear."

In Romans 5:8, Paul says, "But God demonstrated His love to

us, in that while we were still sinners, Christ died for us." So why did Christ have to die for us? Habakkuk 1:12–13 declares, "Are You not from everlasting, O LORD, my God? You are of purer eyes than to behold evil, and cannot look on wickedness."

What then is salvation? Who can be saved? What method does God use to achieve salvation? How can we know that we are saved? What about once saved, always saved? Is it possible to sin so much that God will not save? What is the unforgiveable sin? There are so many questions, yet they all have the same answer. Jesus said, "I Am the way, the truth and the life. No one comes to the Father except through me" (John 14:6).

Jesus saves us. He keeps us saved, and every sin but one sin is forgiven at Calvary. The only sin that is not forgiven is refusing to accept Christ as your Savior. Revelation tells us that at the judgement, every knee will bow, and every tongue will confess that Jesus Christ is Lord. If you wait until then, it will be too late.

There are three tenses of salvation.

1. Past
   I was saved (This occurred at the time of your commitment to Christ). At that time, you were saved from the penalty of your sin.

2. Present
   I am being saved. This is occurring right now as you grow in grace and become a stronger Christian. This is the doctrine of sanctification. It means that as you mature in Christ, you are being saved from the power of sin in your life.

3. Future
   I will be saved. This will occur when we are in heaven, and we will be saved from the very presence of sin.

I am thankful that God's perfect plan for salvation is eternal and that it included me

FOR ME TO LIVE IS CHRIST

For me to live is Christ, to die is gain.
—Philippians 1:31

I n his letter to the Philippians, Paul talked about his life prior to his conversion, his work after salvation, and his great expectations for the future. He talked about being in "a strait bewixt the two" (Philippians 1:23), meaning that his greatest desire was to be with Christ, but he also had a great desire to complete the ministry that he had begun on earth.

Christians need to experience Paul's "straits." The overwhelming, consuming desire of our lives should be to see Jesus. We should long for the day when we can finally lay our crowns at His feet in an act of total adoration and love. We really need to be convinced that "to die is gain" (Philippians 1:31).

On the other hand, we need to have a strong desire to serve Him now. We need to live in a manner that is honoring to God and leads others to know Him too. Regardless of our position in life, we need to make our primary goals consist of spreading the gospel, encouraging fellow believers, building up the church, and living in a way that truly honors God. We need to say as Paul did in Philippians 1:31, "For me to live is Christ."

Then we must commit ourselves to the work that He has given us to do. Let us ask God to increase our faith so that we can serve Him better while keeping our hearts and minds focused on the promise of an eternity that is filled with better things on the day that we finally see our Lord.

In 1984 I wrote the following hymn based on this verse. At the time, my first grandson was gravely ill and we did not know what the outcome would be. Thanks to God's healing grace he grew up to be a wonderful young man. The hymn has been set to music.

FOR ME TO LIVE IS CHRIST

Sometimes the way is dark upon life's pathway.
I cannot see the way God planned for me.
My heart is aching, and my tears fall like raindrops,
But still I'll praise His name for loving me.

And when the way is dim, that's when He nearest;
He calls my name in life's dark hour.
He says, "There's more, My child, than this world's heartaches.
I'm coming soon to take you home with Me."

Oh yes, there's more, my friend, than this world offers.
Christ is the way to live eternally.
Give your heart to Him and trust Him fully.
He wants to give you joy and victory.
Refrain:
For me to live is Christ. O praise His name.
His pledge to me is love. It's always the same.
For me to live is Christ. He never changes.
And when my life is o'er, to die is gain.

GOD CAME TO ME

Yet the Lord will command His loving-kindness in the daytime, and in the night his song shall be with me, and my prayer will be unto the God of my life.
—Psalm 42:8

The psalmist was aware of the presence of the Lord in every circumstance of his life. He honored God, revered Him, and called on Him in every situation. He thanked Him for each blessing, even during difficult situations.

God moves in our lives today and speaks just as clearly as He spoke to David. Too often, we think God doesn't speak to us, but in truth, God spoke, but we weren't listening. Like David, our hearts need to be tune with to Him. In order to hear the voice of God and feel His hand touching us, we must look, listen, and diligently seek to know Him every day of our lives.

We look for instructions from God by studying His Word. His will for us is revealed by thoughtful Bible study, and we will hear Him speaking to us from the pages of the Bible. As we diligently seek the Lord in prayer, He will reveal Himself to us as we study His Word.

We also can see God's work as we observe natural phenomena. The psalmist recognized God as the Creator of all nature and acted upon that knowledge while seeking Him. We also can see God at work as we observe the touch of the Master's hand in our beautiful world.

Today, let us ask God to make our hearts more in tune with Him so that we can see and hear Him in all the ways He chooses to reveal Himself to us. Then let's thank Him for that revelation.

—Tommie McBrayer, 1980

HELP WANTED

Then Jesus said to His disciples, "the harvest truly is plentiful, but the laborers are few. Therefore, pray the Lord of the harvest to send out laborers into His harvest.
—Matthew 9:37–38

Jesus often compared the world to a garden or field in His teachings. He used the parable of the sower, the story of the vineyard, and the passage above, where He issues a call for help with the harvest.

Just as working in a vegetable garden is difficult, time consuming, but necessary if we expect to *reap* a bountiful harvest from that garden, we must also be diligent in our labor if we want reap a harvest in God's garden. Working in a garden demands labor and endurance. It is a continuing chore; it is never finished. Planting seeds, controlling weeds, fertilizing, and watering are necessary. If we expect to have a spiritual harvest, we must do the same thing if we hope to reap the great harvest God has promised.

Just as work in a physical garden helps us develop strength and endurance, work in God's garden builds spiritual strength and endurance. At first, the work seems difficult, but with time and day by day, the work becomes easier. Then as harvest begins, the rich reward makes all the work worthwhile.

So it is in God's garden. As we labor for the Lord, we become stronger spiritually. As we see the Church being edified and encouraged and people coming to know the Lord, we know that our time has been well spent. We cannot know the yield from our harvest until we reach eternity.

The call of Jesus for laborers never ends. It is just as imperative today as it was when He issued that first call for laborers in His vineyard.

My Garden

I walked in my garden this morning
And saw all the things growing there.
They had been lovingly planted, watered, and tended.
They were objects of much tender care.

I walked in my garden this morning,
Removing each weed and each tare,
So that the plants' roots could grow down deep in
the soil
And limbs could reach up to the air.

I gathered my garden this morning,
Garnering its bounty with care.
Each fruit and each flower was a special delight
And a rich reward for my laboring there.

I looked at God's garden this morning.
Millions of people without Christ were there.
The harvest is plentiful, but the laborers are few.
Lord, help me, today, to tell them you care.
—Tommie McBrayer, 1979

HIS EYE IS ON THE SPARROW

Are not two sparrows sold for a penny? Yet not one of them
falls to the ground apart from your Father.
—Matthew 10:29

I used to have a bird feeder in my backyard, just off my patio. I spent many pleasant hours watching the birds that came to the feeder. There were several different kinds of birds: a raucous jay that enjoyed chasing the other birds away, beautiful finches that flittered around and showed off their colorful plumage, and beautiful cooing doves that came and cleared away the seeds that had been scattered on the ground by the other birds. One day, a tiny little sparrow came with three babies that were lined up on the fence waiting to be fed.

I thought about the birds. Each one was very different from the others, but they all ate from the same feeder. Then I thought how they were similar to the people that I know at church. We have finches who are always showing their colors, flitting about, making a beautiful show, and very much interested in the feeder. Then we have the doves: those dependable souls who are busy with mundane but much needed chores around the church. They show up for every service, and they are busy doing mundane chores when no one else is there to see them.

Every now and then, we have a jay that comes in raucously demanding to be seen and sometimes driving others away. Then there are the sparrows. They aren't flashy in their plumage, loud and demanding, or busy with chores, but they always feed with the others. They are dependable, faithful, and more numerous than the others.

Each of the birds comes to the feeder for the same purpose: to feast on the wonderful things that have been provided for them by the person who owns the feeder. The one who provides for the sparrow in our scripture is God. He cares greatly for the sparrows and all the other birds. He cared for you and me enough to send His Son to die for us. What a joy and pleasure it is to come to His feeder and enjoy the bread of life that He provides.

The wonderful gospel hymn "His Eye is on the Sparrow" says it beautifully.

Why should I feel discouraged?
why should the shadows come?
Why should my heart feel lonely?
and long for heaven and home?
When Jesus is my portion,
a constant friend is He,
His eye is on the sparrow,
and I know He watches me.

I rejoice today knowing that I am more valuable to God than the sparrow and that He is truly watching over me.

THE LORD'S PRAYER

MATTHEW 5:9–13

Our Father

The Great I Am who led Moses and the Israelites out of Egypt (see Exodus 3:14)

The Father of Abraham, Isaac, and Jacob (Exodus 3:15)

The eternal God who is the same, "yesterday, today and forever" (Hebrews 13:8)

Who Art in Heaven

The eternal home of the redeemed described by the apostle Paul: "Eye has not seen, nor has ear heard, nor has it entered into the heart of man, what God has in store for His children. (1 Corinthians 2:9)

Hallowed be Thy Name

Hallowed means *holy.* "You be Holy because I am Holy" (Leviticus 11:14; 1 Peter 1:16). This is a command for us to live in a holy way.

"Thou shalt not take the Name of the Lord in Vain" (Exodus 20:7). Do not use the Lord's name in a frivolous and disrespectful way. "There is no other name given under heaven whereby men must be saved."(Acts 4:12)

Thy Kingdom Come

"But seek ye first the kingdom of God" means keeping your focus on Jesus and not on the things of this world (Matthew 6:33). God's spiritual kingdom is here and now in the hearts of those who love Him.

Thy Will Be Done on Earth

God wants people on earth to do His will and practice holy living. When we pray, "Thy will be done," we are asking that *He* fills us with His righteousness and that that righteousness will be reflected in the way we live.

As It Is in Heaven

God's will *is* being done in heaven. There is no sickness, sorrow, pain, death, or sin there. Everything is perfect. We will worship the Lord for eternity in perfect righteousness (see Revelation 21:4–27).

Give Us This Day Our Daily Bread

We are to ask for our *daily* bread, indicating that we want God's provision for today. Tomorrow, we may need to ask again. God is Jehovah Jireh: the God who provides for each day's need. He provided for the Israelites in the wilderness, one day at a time.

And Forgive Us Our Debts

We owed a debt that we could not pay, but Praise God, Jesus paid the price. Paul says in Romans 5:8, "God demonstrated His love to us, that when we were still sinners, Christ died for the ungodly." Our debt was fully paid at Calvary.

As We Forgive Our Debtors

Because God has forgiven us, we are to forgive others, who may have caused us injury or pain. We are to love our neighbors as ourselves. A neighbor is anyone who needs compassion, help, and comfort.

Lead Us Not into Temptation

In Psalm 141:4, David writes, "Incline not my heart to do any evil thing, or to practice wicked works with the workers of iniquity." God does not tempt us to do evil, but Satan certainly will. We must avoid temptation and not succumb to the ways of the world.

But Deliver Us from Evil

Life is a struggle with a powerful enemy. Peter describes him as a roaring lion, seeking whom he may destroy (see 1 Peter 5:8). The Bible also tells us that we have the victory over this adversary: "Greater is He that is in you, than he that is in the world" (1 John 4:4). Thanks be to God who has already provided deliverance for us!

For Thine Is the Kingdom

God's kingdom is eternal. Peter describes our welcome into it: "Entrance will be supplied to you abundantly into the everlasting kingdom of our Lord and Savior Jesus Christ" (2 Peter 1:11).

And the Power and the Glory

After these things I heard a loud voice of a great multitude in heaven saying, "alleluia, salvation and glory and honor and power belong to the Lord our God!" (Revelation 19:1)

Forever

Those who are the redeemed will live forever in that beautiful city, which John describes in Revelation 21 and 22. "Blessed are those who do His commandments, that they may have the right to the tree of life, and may enter through the gates into the city" (Revelation 22:14).

Amen!

The word *amen* literally means *so be it*. Even so, come quickly Lord Jesus!

WHAT IS A GODLY WOMAN?

PROVERBS 31

The Bible has a lot to say about personal holiness in both men and women. The following scriptures speak to this subject. In these passages, the gospel writer is addressing women specifically, but these characteristics apply to all Christians.

1. A godly woman is someone who has experienced repentance, which leads to salvation (see 2 Corinthians 7:10). Without salvation by grace through faith, no person can be godly.
2. The godly woman will live "self-controlled, and upright ... in this present age" (Titus 2:12).
3. A godly woman controls her speech. She is not a gossip, and she does not use profanity and unwholesome speech (see Ephesians 4:29).
4. A godly woman dresses modestly and adorns herself with good deeds, which are appropriate for women who profess to worship God (see 1 Timothy 2:9–10).
5. A godly woman is not fooled by the lies that try to convince her that her worth is determined by elements of physical beauty (see 1 John 5:19). Rather, she focuses on inner beauty, which reflects her relationship with Christ.
6. A godly woman lives in purity and reverence (1 Peter 3:2).
7. The godly woman is industrious, taking care of her household, honoring her husband, and working diligently to provide for her family. According to Proverbs 31, she is more valuable than rubies.

The Bible is replete with women who exhibited these characteristics. Deborah was the leader of Israel and commander in chief of its military. She led the army into battle. Ruth was a gentile who served God with her whole heart. We see her devotion to her mother-in-law, Naomi. She was one of two women who are included in the genealogy of Jesus. Hannah was consistent and persistent in her prayer for a son. God answered her prayer, and the prophet Samuel was born.

There are many New Testament women of note. The woman at the well (John 4) was a social outcast who had been married many times. There was Priscilla, who was the wife of Aquila. Joanna was a member of Caesar's household and a follower of Christ. Elizabeth was the cousin of Mary. Mary was the mother of Jesus. Paul mentions Lydia, a businesswoman, who allowed Paul to establish a church in her house. The daughters of Philip were evangelists. Many others are mentioned by Paul in his letters to the churches.

Godly women today have many opportunities to help in the Great Commission's task of bringing the gospel to the world. It starts with our families, extends to our neighbors, and applies in our churches and through our missions' activities and opportunities. I am thankful that God blessed me with a mother who exhibited many of these qualities.

TRIBUTE TO MOTHER

(In Memory of My Mother, Sarah Lilly Smith, June 10, 1919–June 4, 1990)

A woman of God is a special creation.
Her heart is often filled with joy and elation,
As she views all around and observes in her space,
God's wonderful touch of mercy and grace.

A woman of God is a creature of beauty.
Her life, filled with love, is more than mere duty.
Her husband and children all call her blessed.
She honors them all,
Although tried and tested.

A woman of God is busy each day,
Helping, working, and showing others the way.
She shares her joy and radiant faith,
Which is a reflection of God's goodness and grace.

A woman of God is more than just mother.
Her children adore her, but there is another
Reason that she is such a beautiful being.
Her life is in Christ and He is seeing
A person of wisdom,
Who has placed in His hands,
Her family, home, children, and man.

God, grant me the grace to be that kind of woman.
Let my life be a blessing wherever I am.
Let my husband, my children, and all others who
know me
Understand that the peace and joy that I have in living
Is a gift from above that comes from believing,
And let me teach to my daughter that a woman
should be
All of those things my mother taught me.
—Tommie McBrayer, 1991

A THOUGHT FOR EASTER

APRIL 2020

> Jesus spoke these words, lifted up His eyes to heaven, and said: "Father, the hour has come. Glorify Your Son, that Your Son also may glorify You. ... I have manifested Your name to the men who You have given Me ... They were Yours. You gave them to Me, and they have kept Your word. I pray for ... those whom You have given me, for they are Yours. ... I do not pray for these alone, but also for those who will believe in Me through their word."
>
> —John 17:1–20

Easter is such a special time because of our Savior's redemptive act at Calvary. We read and hear a lot about the cross and His suffering. But did you know He prayed for you before He went to the cross?

In my study, I have been reading and remembering the prayer that Jesus said in John 17. He and his disciples had just finished observing the Passover in the upper room, and they were walking across the Kidron Valley to Gethsemane. Jesus was teaching them some very important things as they walked.

Then he begins to pray. "Father, the hour has come. Glorify Your Son, that Your son may glorify You" (John 17:1). The prayer continues in verse 9. Jesus says," I pray for them. I do not pray for the world." In verse 11, He prays, "I am no longer in the world, and I come to you, Father, keep through Your name those whom You have given Me, that they may be one with You" (John 17:1–21).

Jesus makes nine requests for his followers in this prayer. He was praying for his disciples, but His prayer transcends all time. The prayer is for you and me, just as much as it was for John, Peter, and the rest of the disciples. How humble I feel when I think that Jesus prayed for me while he was on His way to the cross.

Get your Bible and read the entire chapter, focusing on the verses that express a prayer for you from the heart of Jesus (verses 11, 13, 15, 17, 20, 21, 23, 24, and 26). These all have a prayer for the followers of Jesus. There is an old country, gospel song, "When He was on the cross, I was on His mind, written by Ronnie Hinson and Mike Payne, tells us beautifully exactly what this passage means.

He is Risen!

HE KNOWS MY NAME!

But Jesus said to her "Mary!" She turned and said to Him
"Rabboni!" (which is to say Teacher).
—John 20:16

In John 20, we find Mary Magdalene going to the tomb to anoint the body of Jesus. She went to the tomb early in the morning and on the first day of the week. To her great surprise, she found an empty tomb. The stone that had been placed at the door of the tomb and then sealed with the Roman seal had been rolled away.

There in the garden, Mary began to weep. She thought someone had stolen the body of Jesus. She did not know that He had been resurrected and that He was no longer dead. He was alive!

There was a man in garden who spoke to Mary. She did not recognize him and thought he must be the gardener.

He said, "Woman, why are you weeping? Whom are you seeking?"

Mary said, "Because they have taken away my Lord, and I do not know where they have laid Him and I will take Him away."

Jesus said to her "Mary!

She turned and said to Him, "'Rabboni', (which is to say Teacher.)" (John 20:15–16).

In John 10:14, we read that about Jesus comparing Himself to a good shepherd who calls his sheep by name. He knows the name of every one of those sheep. The passage says, "I am the good shepherd; and I know My sheep, and am known by them … and other sheep I have which are not of this fold; them also I must bring, and they will hear My voice and there will be one flock."

Reverend C. Austin Miles was a hymnist who had just read the account of Mary meeting the risen Christ. He was so moved by what happened to Mary. He thought that this was not just something she had experienced two thousand years ago. It was something for all Christians in every age. Jesus knows our name, and when we seek Him, He will come to us just as He came to Mary all those years ago. The beautiful hymn "In the Garden" was written by Reverend Miles in 1912, in response to his experience that day. I pray it is ours as well.

In the Garden

I come to the garden alone,
while the dew is still on the roses,
And the voice I hear, falling on my ear,
the Son of God discloses.

He speaks and the sound of His voice
Is so sweet the birds hush their singing,
And the melody he gave to me, within my heart is ringing.

I'd stay in the garden with Him,
tho' the night around me be falling,
But He bids me go, thro' the voice of woe,
His voice to me iscalling.

Refrain

And He walks with me, And He talks with me,
And He tells me I am His own,
And the joy we share, as we tarry there,
None other has ever known.
—C. Austin Miles, 1912

PEACE, PEACE

God will keep those in perfect peace, whose mind is focused on Him.
> —Isaiah 26:3 (paraphrased by the author)

And suddenly there was with the angel a multitude of the heavenly host praising God and saying: Glory to God in the highest, and on earth peace, goodwill toward men.
> —Luke 2:13–14

Peace I leave with you, My peace I give to you; not as the world gives do I give it to you.
> —John 14:11

The Christmas story shares about the angels telling the message of peace to the shepherds. It is one of the most familiar passages regarding the birth of the Christ child, and it is found in Luke. Christ is the one whom Isaiah called the, "Prince of Peace" (Isaiah 9:6).

As I said before, I was studying Isaiah 26:3. I learned that the Hebrew word for *peace* actually means *peace, peace*. It is a double portion of God's peace. What a wonderful promise! God's peace, peace is available for people who keep their hearts and minds on Him.

In today's world, there isn't much peace. Nations are at war with each other. We are in the midst of a worldwide pandemic, and many people are experiencing panic but not peace. Our media contributes to the feeling of panic because of their constant negative reporting on the situation. Our political leaders are trying to manage a situation that is really beyond their control.

Some people say God is punishing an unbelieving and immoral world because of their sin, just as He did in biblical days. Others say that this is a naturally occurring phenomenon, the likes of which we have not experienced in more than one hundred years. It is impossible to know the origins of the disease or the ultimate outcome. There is no one to blame.

I know one thing for certain: The Bible is our ultimate hope. The Bible uses the phrases "Do not be afraid," and, "Fear not," 365 times. God is in control. Once for every day in the year!

I wrote the following poem during Desert Storm, our first war in the Middle East. It focuses on peace from all sources and of every kind. It is still very relevant today.

ATTITUDE OF THE HEART

If I could stop the bombs from falling
And destroy all the materials of war,
I could not bring peace,
For peace is not the absence of global conflict.
It is an attitude of the heart
That allows nations, large and small
And of every political persuasion
To determine together those policies that bring about
The universal good for all mankind.

If I could stop the violence in our cities
And destroy the evil mentality that leads to drive-by killings
And the rape of our children,
I could not bring peace,
For peace is not the absence of hostility in our streets.
It is an attitude of the heart
That compels persons of every color, race, and religion
To live side by side and in harmony.

If I could end the mindless hypocrisy
That divides churches and destroys denominations,
I could not bring peace,
For peace is not the saccharine-sweet
Super piety of some religious people, institutions, and entities.
It is an attitude of the heart
That binds individuals and entities together in love
And ushers us into the very presence of God.

THE HOLY CITY,
THE NEW JERUSALEM

Now I, John, saw the holy city, New Jerusalem, coming down out of heaven from God, prepared as bride for her husband. And I heard a loud voice from heaven saying, "Behold, the tabernacle of God is with men, and He will dwell with them, and they shall be His people. God Himself will be with them and be their God. And God will wipe away every tear from their eyes; there shall be no more death, nor sorrow, nor crying. There shall be no more pain, for the former things have passed away."
—Revelation 21:2–4

There are several basic things to know about this "Holy City."

1. It is a community of believers. No one who has rejected Jesus Christ as Savior will be there.
2. It is a gift of God. John says, "Coming down out of heaven from God."
3. It is the eternal dwelling place that Jesus promised us in John 14.
4. It is called a "bride," indicating our relationship with Jesus in eternity. The bride is pure, spotless, and totally committed to her groom.
5. It is God's permanent dwelling place. God first dwelt with Israel in a tent (tabernacle) so that it could be moved from place to place. John tells us that the Word (Jesus) became flesh and dwelt (tabernacled) among us. We experience the very presence

of God now in our lives, but in the Holy City, we will see Him face to face.

6.   It is a place where all things will be made *new*. Paul tells us that when we are "in Christ," we are a "new creation" (2 Corinthians 5:17). In delivering sermon on this topic, a pastor of mine defined it as "another of a totally different kind." This is something that has never been before. We are completely changed from our old selves to our new selves. We are new creations, and the world that we will enter will not be like anything on earth today.

7.   It is perfect in its
    a.   dimensions (a perfect cube of approximately 1,500 feet),
    b.   beauty (everything there is perfect),
    c.   provision for our needs (every need is supplied),
    d.   fellowship (we will all worship and praise the same Savior), and
    e.   worship (no atheists or worshippers of idols will be there).

8.   It is our eternal home. Where will we live, and what will we do there? Can we take anything with us? I believe we can.

In John 14:1–3, Jesus said,

> Let not your heart be troubled, you believe in God, believe also in me. In my Father's house there are many mansions (dwelling places), if it were not so, I would have told you. And if I go to prepare a place for you, I will come again and receive you to Myself; that where I am, there you may be also.

Heaven is where Jesus has prepared a dwelling place for us. It is a wonderful place where we will experience God's everlasting love throughout eternity. It is also a place where we will be with our families, our children, our spouses, and others that we have known and loved.

We will be there for eternity, enjoying God's love for us and experiencing a transcendent human love, which will go with us to that wonderful place. I believe this transcendent love, like God's love, is everlasting, but it is higher, deeper, and broader in scope than anything we have experienced on earth. I believe we will share that great love throughout eternity in our dwelling place. I am looking forward to the day when I can experience this love that transcends time and space with those loved ones who are, even now, dwelling in that perfect place.

NOTES

Printed in the United States
By Bookmasters